MW01029805

The Murder of
William Marsh Rice

The Murder of William Marsh Rice

A Galveston Storm Novel

Paul N. Spellman

This is a work of historical fiction.

Except for three major characters, every named person in this story is real.

Every place and event is a recounting exactly as it occurred.

P. S.

Preface

On September 8, 1900, a hurricane raged across Galveston Island off the coast of Texas, destroying the island city. Over 6,000 lost their lives in the deadliest natural disaster in American history.

On January 10, 1901, Lucas Well No. 1 blew in two miles south of Beaumont, Texas, at Spindletop, ushering in the greatest petroleum boom in the history of the United States.

These singular events, only sixteen weeks apart, mark the most important epoch in Texas history since the Revolution of 1836.

In late September, 1900, Texas philanthropist William Marsh Rice was found dead in his New York City apartment. An investigation into his death ensued.

Prologue

The shadow moved slowly, carefully down the long hall, pausing every few steps, listening. The floorboards creaked and the noise seemed to echo through the apartment. The thin young man held an armful of supplies for the job he was about to begin. He passed two other doors, then stopped at the third. It was already cracked open about six inches, the way he had left it an hour earlier. He nudged his shoulder gently against the panel and the door swung open. Except for the whisper against the carpet it made no other sound.

He was on safer ground now - no more wooden floor to contend with. The darkness enveloped him, but his eyes had become used to the blackness that surrounded him, and besides, he knew his way around this room well enough to have been blindfolded, which is what it felt like at that moment.

Now he heard the soft breathing noises coming from the other side of the room. They were interspersed with a crackly snore, which meant the old man was deep in sleep. Good. Three steps, pause, three more, stop. He stood at the bedside.

Carefully now, he placed the supplies on the carpeted floor at the side of the bed. He had practiced this only once, some hours earlier, but it hadn't seemed very difficult then. But his hands had not been trembling then; now they shook as if he had the palsy. He balled his fingers into fists, gripped them tightly to make the trembling go away. It didn't work. He interlaced his fingers, plied them together like he was kneading bread. That helped. A little.

A minute had passed since he entered the room. Enough time wasted, he chastised himself silently. He bent down, picked up the large towel that was neatly folded, let it fall out of its fold as he raised it up. He draped it over one arm, reached back down and picked up the glass jar, quietly twisted the metal cap off, shoved the cap into his pants pocket. The smell came quickly. Why didn't I do this before I came in here, he complained to himself. Oh well. Finish it.

The man poured half of the contents of the jar, about a goblet full, onto a small sponge that lay on the towel, letting it soak in. He put the jar down on the floor. Twisted the towel into the shape of a cone, roughly, closed at its top and splayed out in folds at the bottom. The soaking sponge he placed on the opening at the top of the cone.

Now was the moment. He gulped, realized he hadn't taken a breath in awhile, inhaled deeply. Once. One more. He stared through the darkness at the features of the face that lay on the pillow. Craggy, frail, he knew the color was pale, the thinned hair disheveled. The old man was dying - slowly - too slowly.

The shadowy figure laid the towel and sponge over the old man's head, letting it rest on the pillow. He brought it down over his victim in slow motion, until he felt its weight come to rest. He pulled his hands back. The cone held its shape. He took a step back from the bed, from the moment. From the crime.

Reached down. Picked up the jar, the lid still in his pocket. Took steps backward, still facing the bed. Drew his hand behind him, groping for the opened door. Stepped back out into the hallway. Turned to his left. Walked quickly now to the bathroom at the corner of the long hall. Stepped inside, shut the door. Why? Washed his hands. Rinsed out the jar. Sniffed at its opening. Rinsed it again.

He stepped out into the hall, took another left, walked briskly into the sitting room, into its darkness. Felt for the leather high-backed chair that had stood in its place for a year. Sat down.

Thirty minutes, he thought to himself. I am to wait thirty minutes. A million years.

"Is it done?" The low voice came from somewhere across the room, startling the young man, who gulped and sat up straight. His stomach churned. He pressed his thighs together to prevent an accident. "Is it done?" The voice repeated the question, calmly, slowly.

"Yes."

A million years go by.

The thin man stood from his chair when he had had enough of the wait, the interminable silence. He could only hear the breathing of the other man, the one in the darkness sitting over there somewhere. It drove him crazy. It must be thirty minutes, he convinced himself. Turning out of the room, he walked carefully, aware of each stride he took, thinking maybe he walked along a precipice now. One wrong step and a fall. Or maybe the fall had already begun.

He reached the door still cracked open, pushed it gently with just one finger of his left hand. Listened. No sound. No snore. No breathing. Deathly silent, he mused grimly. Stepped inside. Closed the door, wondered why he did that.

He covered the distance to the bedside. Stood there, letting his eyes get accustomed to this special darkness. The vague outline of the towel emerged gradually. The smell was strong from the sponge. He lifted the two items off the old man's face, held each in a hand, outstretched from him as if disclaiming. Peered down between his arms to the gray face. Then, in what would have been seen as a ridiculous pose had anyone else – alive – been there, the shadow bent at the waist, lowering his head toward the figure on the bed while leaving his arms stretched out. Like he was preparing to leap from a cliff, soar off to…Hell.

His face inches from the other's, the young valet closed his eyes and waited for some noise of life. Some sense of existence. Some way to tell that perhaps it could all be turned around. Time pushed back. Another alternative.

But there was nothing. A lifeless body lay in the bed.

So. It was done.

Part One

Galveston, September 8, 1900, 6:00 A.M.

Fourteen Days Earlier

1

I was sitting at a poker table on the second floor of the Tremont Hotel, thinking I could help clean up the city if I shot the fellow sitting across from me. It was just before dawn and we had been playing for six hours. I had him for over $1,200 at the time and he was desperate enough to be dealing from the bottom of the deck. I didn't think anyone in the Galveston police department would mind if I killed him: less stupidity within the city limits.

Anyway, that was when I felt the storm. I didn't see it or hear it yet, just felt it coming. I got up and walked over to the window, drew the heavy, lace drape aside and stared out across the downtown buildings. It was first light, and the shadows were still winning. I couldn't make out any of the storefront signs. But I was looking past them, staring south out into the darkness that

I knew was the Gulf. I glared so hard at the inky nothing that my head throbbed after a few moments.

I don't know how long I stood there. The fellow at the table could have picked up my chips and been halfway to New Orleans for all I knew. Or cared. I was staring all the way back to 1886.

⸺⸻⸺

I had ridden hard all morning across the Montana hillside. Tom Horn and Sebio were long since gone, gone down to Arizona, I think, to hunt Apaches with the Rangers. Or maybe the other way around. Didn't matter. They always found trouble. We'd been in trouble in Wyoming back in the fall, come up to Montana for the winter, hired on to move some cattle up to a high meadow for the spring. Now it was March, the 15th.

"Beware the Ides of March," my Momma used to tell me in the spring. She'd get this strange, dark and funny look in her eyes, shift them around like she was watching for a stranger's ears to be too near. Her voice would get real low, lower than it already was, and she'd half-whisper, "Beware the Ides of March." I'd freeze like a statue - it became part of the game, I suppose - and then she'd kiss me on the cheek and I'd hug her real tight around the neck, like I was afraid and that would help somehow.

I don't remember ever being afraid, not then, not since.

So I'd been left with ninety head of stringy winter cattle, a chuck wagon and two stupid mules, and ten more miles. I had hired three boys, I think the oldest couldn't have been more than fifteen, to help finish the drive, but two of them were dumber than the mules, and the three of them had already cleaned out the wagon of all except some coffee and flour.

The weather had already broken, maybe ten days earlier, but clouds had come in during the night, and now it was raining. It was a cold rain, and it was running off my hat and directly down my back inside the duster. No matter how I shifted on the back of my palomino, the rain found the inside of my shirt.

The wind shifted about two hours into day, straight out of the north, and hard, brittle. The rain quit long enough for nothing to dry good, and then the snow started. It was mixed up with some sleet that must have come off one of the glaciers my mother used to read to me about, like somebody was firing nails out of a two-pounder right at my face. My bandana was long since drenched and worthless, but I wrapped it across my mouth anyway. Senseless.

I couldn't see the boys anywhere. Hell, I couldn't see my horse's nose, it was so wet and white around me. I figured they'd headed for the wagon. They never were very far from it most of the time.

The wind picked up and I could hear the whistling, like a train just over the rise. I turned my mount right into the teeth of the storm, my head down on the nape of his neck. I gave him the reins, just trying to hold on. He wandered off to the right some, and I felt us going down an incline, into a creek bed maybe. He wandered us right against the wall that rose up along the dry creek, and a sliver of stone tore through my pants leg just above my boot. I was so cold I could hardly feel it, but when I reached down to touch it I winced a bit. I pulled my glove right up close and saw the blood. Well, damn. I didn't suppose I'd die from it, so I just held tight to my mount and shut my eyes against the storm.

I guess we stayed there a couple hours. Could've been the rest of the month, I don't know. About mid-afternoon the storm let up just long enough for me to ride up onto the prairie and take a look around.

Everywhere I looked was white. Maybe four inches, five, had already fallen. The wind was just takin its own breath for a spell, but the clouds told me we weren't near finished. I spotted three head of cattle way off to the west, but nothing else was out there. I left them to figure out what to do. I was doing the same.

The storm hit again, and then at dark once more. I had burrowed up against the rim of the creekbed wall, kinda digging out a little cave where I could lie flat and low. I took my saddle and blanket off and let the horse go on. He had a better chance without me hanging all over him.

Once, way after midnight I guessed, there was a break in the gray-black clouds, and I counted a handful of stars peeking down to see if anyone was left alive. I didn't feel it.

It was snowing at daybreak, and the whistle coming over the plains was a howl. Like a wolf running down elk, just always moving and never giving up, making that low growling sound that gave the jacks nightmares. Never giving up.

I have since forgotten how long it iced and swirled on that prairie. Doesn't matter anymore. When it stopped, the temperature had dropped below freezing, and there was maybe two feet of snow everywhere. Drifts curled up twelve, 15 feet into the air, making dancing patterns over the prairie. Looked like a desert with its dunes going clear to the horizon in every direction.

I had ice hanging off every part of me. Blood caked down my leg into the toes of my boot. I was cramped up and felt like a hundred years old, not 21 anymore. The storm had just aged me, just like that. Helluva thing. I rolled out of my cave home and took a minute to uncork myself and stand up. The Ute blanket was stiff as a board on my back. I let it drop to the ground. The sun broke through the leftover clouds, but there wasn't any heat coming from it. Just bright. A lot of bright off that snow, made me shut my eyes and cuss.

My horse was gone for now, and I was too cold to whistle for him. I walked about a hundred yards just to see if I could, and looked around again. Nothing for miles but white. Two hundred more yards, this time to my left - west, I guessed. I headed south for a rise so I could see better, another mile or so. Got up on top of it. A tumbleweed raced me the last few steps, and won. It must have come from Alaska. It was gone before I could ask.

I looked out over winter come late, come hard. It was five minutes before my eyes could focus far enough to spot the chuck wagon. Back off to the east and north a bit, maybe three miles. Well, a walk'd warm me up.

When I saw him I was still ten paces from the wagon. The tarp had been ripped off its moorings, and wooden braces were sticking straight up in the cold air, like a giant prickly pear. Frozen. The snow was up over *the rim, and a drift of the stuff had thrown itself up over one side, where I thought the barrel of flour might still be tied off. There was no sound. Even the wind had gone off somewhere to look for trouble.*

His hand was raised in the air, his fingers splayed out wide, his arm slightly crooked at the elbow. His shirt sleeve had frozen against his wrist, but a little corner of it waved in the leftover breeze. There was ice gathered on the back of each finger, like a makeshift glove that he had put on at the last. I leaned over the side and followed the line of the stiff arm down into the bed of the wagon.

He was on his back, his eyes staring long past me or anything else. His blue lips were curled in an angry smile. I remember his name was Will.

Never found the others.

I watched the first glimmer of day out the window at the Tremont. The clouds were mostly broken and confused. Two Negro men walked out from a warehouse down below and over one street. One of them was carrying a heavy sack over one shoulder, kind of bent him over. They were both talking, I couldn't hear 'em but the one with the sack was shaking his head real hard and the other one was waving his arms in response. They were walking at an easy gait, sure of where they were headed. Probably same as every day. Saturday made no nevermind to them.

There was a flag hanging limp on top of a building, maybe the post office. I hadn't been in Galveston but a few weeks, didn't much know my way around. I'd found the Deepwater Saloon and the Tremont where I stood, and knew which way were the docks, the Midway, the train station. I could eat, drink, sleep, trade, or leave without too much trouble.

I stared at that flag for awhile longer. Dawn, an island city on the Gulf, uncertain sky, and not a breath of wind? When I'd been in Cuba two years before, the wind always blew on the coast except twice. Both times in '98 the wind stopped dead, then whorled itself up like a cobra and spit the damnedest hurricanes at that island you can imagine. Just like the '86 storm. No reason. No warning. No stopping it.

"Damn," I said, out loud I guess because someone behind me answered. "What?" "Storm coming up today," I replied to the voice. "Ah, hell," the voice spit, "Storms always coming in here. No big deal. No big deal."

I walked outside a few minutes later, having cashed in my chips and reclaimed my jacket from a girl who wore a lot of pink. The temperature said I wouldn't need the jacket soon, but the morning still suggested it.

I was hungry. I'd eaten my last four meals at the Tremont, so a change seemed in order. I found a restaurant two doors away, sat at a corner table in the back, and ordered coffee and bacon. A gracious woman well-worn but happy brought me my coffee, and the bacon smothered in biscuits and gravy and grits. Two men in black suits sat at the table in front by the window, my only meal-time companions. They glanced outside every once in awhile, but I don't know if they saw what I had seen. Trouble coming.

I left before they did, nodding at the hostess on my way out into the street. I took a cross street and headed for the Gulf side of the island. It was nearly eight o'clock, and a few folks were stirring. A man drove by on a bicycle, had some packages in a basket in front of him. He rode too slowly, and the front wheel kept waving on him. He'd fling the handlebars at that wheel and correct his direction, then slip off the sidewalk and repeat the maneuver. Seemed to me like he'd take forever to get where he was going that way. Maybe he didn't care where he was going. I didn't.

I heard a baby crying from one of the houses as I walked by. It had an eerie wail that drifted out an open window and onto the street. Kinda lay there on the bricks, no breeze to blow it on. The baby'd cry real hard, then cough, catch its breath with a little *hmph*, then take up the wail again. Just as I crossed a street away from the house, I thought I heard a snatch of music. The mother's lullaby. My momma used to sing to me all the time, made-up songs about puppies and blueberry cakes and springtime.

I looked out over what they called the Midway. Mostly some ramshackles, three or four strutted out on piers, bath houses strewn around the beach like toy boxes. The trolley track ran right into the middle of the jumble, sitting up about six feet on its dike, curving back toward the city and disappearing between some homes. Right in the middle of that section of beach was what was left of a pier, much bigger than the others even as ruined as it was now. One piece of leftover wall still hung at a strange angle from the pier moorings. I'd heard there'd been a great hotel there once, until a storm tore it to pieces. I thought maybe that wall was a warning. The Midway didn't seem concerned.

I turned to head back into town. Some children ran past me, laughing and racing each other to the water. I heard some giggles and some splashing, but I didn't look back.

Another block towards downtown, and I stopped in my tracks. Sensed it starting. A moment passed. The wind arrived on the street where I stood, ambling alongside me at first, but it had an anger in it. Some rain suggested itself on the lapel of my coat, and I pulled my hat brim forward a bit, hunched my shoulders instinctively, started walking. I didn't hurry. That seemed unnecessary somehow, like it didn't matter how much anybody hurried over the next few hours, the storm was gonna overtake us anyway.

By the time I arrived back at the Tremont, the wind was picking up and the rain was harder. Nobody in the foyer seemed the least bit interested in that signal information, so I didn't bother sharing it. Kept my coat on, handed my hat to the pink girl, and sidled onto a bar stool, asked Emmitt for coffee. He was bald and heavyset, probably my age but looked older. He had an easy smile, but in a pinch I believe he'd be handy to have on my side. His forearms looked like fence posts, his hands wide and thick fingers. He liked to brush his right hand over the top of his head just before saying something, like some part of him still recalled a head of hair needing mending. Nothing there now, though.

I said thanks when the coffee appeared in front of me, and he mumbled nothing. Smiled. I decided to try out my pearl of wisdom on Emmitt. "Rainin," I announced. "Big storm gonna come up."

"Yeah?" He patted down his head.

"Hm mm," I replied knowledgeably. He stared past me for a minute, out the barroom window and onto the street. The rain was skittering against the window canopy, starting to form little waterfalls. A gust of wind careened against the canopy and the waterfalls vanished, then returned.

"So, Mr. Lincoln," Emmitt spoke up in a friendly tone. I appreciated his remembering my name from a previous conversation. "Job bring you down this way, huh?"

"Cale," I said. "Friends call me Cale."

Emmitt nodded, then looked down into my coffee cup, like it was a gypsy's ball maybe, turned and walked down to the end of the bar. He brushed his hand over his head, and bent over elbows down on the mahogany surface. Laced his hammy fingers together in front of him. I guessed our stimulating conversation was over for now.

I put some coins on the bar by the coffee cup and walked back outside, retrieving my hat and gaining a pink smile as a bonus. I stood on the sidewalk, under a wide rafter, watched the rain get more determined, the wind get angrier. I had no idea what to do next, so I thought about leaving the island. If I went on into Houston on the ten o'clock train, maybe I could get ahead of this storm, and go see Mr. Rice if he was around.

William Marsh Rice had hired me back in August to keep an eye on his warehouse over on the bayou. There'd been some break-ins, and Mr. Rice living in New York City most of every year thought some security might be necessary. I had met him briefly in New York in the spring at a big banquet he threw for some of the war veterans back from Havana. I'd come home with T.R. and some of the others in the frontier battalion, got my old job back with Pinkerton's, and thought I might just settle into some big city living.

We were all pretty tired of fighting, of jungles and hill climbing and killing, and the heat and the heavy wet air. The city looked pretty good. The colonel put a word in for me at the banquet, and Mr. Rice asked me if I would be interested in going to Houston. Said he'd heard good things about me, needed a good man he could trust. That kinda talk. He was old and shriveling, but his voice was steady. Not loud. There was something about him I just took to, first time he shook my hand. He was boney-fingered, but the handshake was firm, meant business.

By the end of the banquet he had himself a Houston security chief.

He likely was back in New York by now, but I thought it might be as good an excuse as any to get off the island for the time being. Storms don't treat island cities kindly, I supposed.

I headed for the train station. It was close to ten o'clock. The rain and the wind were fighting each other now, bucking and kicking the hell out of everything they rammed into. Two giants beating the crap out of each other, running and falling and wrestling, knocking down store signs and people. The storm didn't care. Just kept struggling. Maybe it wanted to lift the whole island up out of the water and toss it halfway across Texas. I thought maybe it could.

I got my own licks in as I cut my way through the streets, leaning heavily against the walls of the buildings, sometimes grappling from brick to door sill to post, like I was climbing sideways along a cliff.

I gave up on staying dry. My hat had long since started for Houston ahead of me, and I pulled my coat up over my ears. Kept going. There may have been other people on that street, I wasn't paying attention. I heard some shouts but they were caught in the howling wind and could've come from anywhere.

I came to an intersection, which meant I'd have to leave the cover of the buildings while I crossed over. Not a pleasant thought. I took one step away from the bricked corner. The bicycle hit me right in my left kidney, dropped me into the street like a boxer diving for the canvas. I flung my hands out to catch myself, and they slammed against the brick street at the same instant my head went under water. A fleeting thought suggested I should be grateful for the water breaking my fall. Uh huh.

I came up on my hands and knees, soaked through, shaking my head to clear it of the pain and the water. I considered reaching for my pistol and taking out the bike rider where he stood. Seemed fair. But the pain kept me doubled over and not at my best.

"Sorry," a voice hollered through the storm. It was right in my ear, but I could barely make out the word anyway. I twisted my head around and looked right in the attacker's face. I probably looked frightening. He recoiled about ten inches. Then he smiled. "Cale?"

It was Isaac Cline who'd bore down on me with that damn machine of his. I hadn't seen Isaac in eighteen months, back outside of Guatemala City. He was working on a cure for the malaria, hired by the U. S. Army, had a lab going down there in the jungle that Walter Reed had put up. I was just out of Santiago, taking the long route back to the States after cleaning up some things we left undone there.

"Isaac!" I hollered back in his face. He grabbed me by my coat and pulled me to my feet. I was ankle deep in the puddle of swirling muck, and my back hurt. "What the hell you doing here?"

"Cale Lincoln, you son-of-a-bitch, I work here!" he answered back in a shout. "Doing the weather on the island. We got a bad one going here!" I nodded my head, stepped onto the sidewalk and grabbed him by the arm to get my balance. He left the bicycle laying there and we crammed up against a wall out of the wind.

"And what the hell are you doing here?" he asked back at me. I shouted in his ear about working for Rice at his warehouse, taking some casual time in Galveston. "Nice place to visit!" I finished.

The wind roared and cut off our conversation, slammed us hard against the bricks. It felt like some kind of strange gravity pull, neither of us could move. We were two blocks from the docks on 24th Street, and the train station somehow seemed a million miles away. Getting there and getting off this fool island seemed now a remote possibility.

The roar stuttered just a moment, and I grabbed Isaac by his coat sleeve, pulled him around the corner and inside a door. We both stumbled in the dry, still air, caught ourselves. Fell into two chairs squeezed into what looked like someone's office. Didn't say a word for maybe two minutes. The roar was dulled but still winning outside.

"Cale, I'm really worried about this one," Cline finally broke the eerie silence. "I've been tracking it on the Morse since Monday. They say it hit over by Cuba, maybe Puerto Rico got it, too. Fella in New Orleans" - he pronounced it the natives' way -"got an SOS from two steamers out in the Gulf. When he tried to get back with them, nobody answered." I nodded. "This one's coming like a locomotive, Cale," he concluded, "nothing to stop it."

"What can I do for you, Isaac?" I asked. "I ain't going anywhere, looks like."

"Dunno, Cale," he replied." I gotta get the word around, if it's not too late already." He stared out the small office window for a moment, took a deep breath. "People gotta get off the streets, get in the big buildings, get outa the beach homes. This thing's not near over yet."

"Well, let's split up," I suggested. "Where were you headed?"

"I've been over to the *News,* sent a fella to the station and another to the Y. My brother is working his way the other end of Market Street, says he could get to the hospital, he'll stay there and ride it out." He paused, visualizing the city streets. "Lucas Terrace needs to clear out."

"Where's that?"

"Over off Broadway, east near the Midway," he half-pointed in that general direction. "That end of the island's gonna get it worst."

"You want me to go out there?"

"Yeah. No, let me. I know where it is. Why don't you head up the island? If you stay along Market, the buildings'll hold off the wind, you can make some good time mebbe."

"All right," I said. We sat for another minute, didn't say a word, just stared at each other. I got up out of my chair, reached for his outstretched hand, shook it hard, and walked out the door, turned left, headed west. Didn't look back.

Nice day for a walk.

2

Walking was a relative term. I pulled myself along walls, darted inside doorways whenever possible, scratched and crawled and ran across the intersections.

The water was running the streets now, ankle deep on Market, higher down the island. The clouds were black and darkness covered the city. Rooftops cracked so loud that it sounded like cannon shot coming from high on a hilltop somewhere. A wall would collapse, and the echo would bounce and scream and bounce again, finally drowning in a pool of swirling debris.

Glass and brick and wooden planks lay everywhere. I had to climb one pile to get past and ripped a crimson gash right across my neck. I kept pushing through, absent-mindedly wrapping the wound with a handkerchief.

There were people in the streets, and some looking out from windows, scared witless, their eyes all white and ready to die. On 34th Street I watched five children playing in a muddied park, rolling a hoop along until the wind sent it airborne. They chased it for fifty yards, laughing and pointing and shoving each other to be the first to grab it when it landed.

It didn't. Caught in a tree, jammed there. I stopped for a moment to catch whatever breath I might still have, and watched them from the sidewalk. There was a boom and a crack, the echo slammed into me in a split second, just as I saw a huge limb break away from its moorings above the children. I tried to shout and tried to move, but nothing responded the way it was supposed to. I froze. The children looked up, then shrunk back in the same instant. The limb glanced off a smaller branch before it struck, knocking two of the children to the ground.

A third one put her hands to her face and screamed. I could hear that above all the storm's noise. It jerked me into moving, and I ran across the park, sliding to a halt in the mud and bending down to grab the limb. The other children had run off, except the screaming girl who stood there and did that. The limb was heavy in the rain but I managed to lift it and move it.

Both the children stared at me, dead. One had his head tilted awkwardly, his neck broken. The other was crushed from shoulder to waist.

I picked the boy up first, stood and looked around. Someone was running from a nearby building, and then others right behind. The first man there took the child in my arms and headed up the street; the others took the dead girl and the screaming girl away.

I just stood there for awhile. I pulled my pistol out from under my coat and vest, and shot the limb. Once. Walked away.

I walked due south for six blocks, deliberately into the punishing hurricane, hoping the pain and the wet would somehow drive the picture of those two kids from my memory. Didn't help. The water was rising quickly now where I pushed against the storm, knee deep in most places, higher in others. Rivers flowed freely into the houses that I passed. Up stairs and onto porch fronts. Smaller buildings floated by, or were dashed against the larger homes. Crushed and splintered lumber stacked up everywhere. Pieces of glass — windows? — rushed along the canal streets, cutting and tearing at whatever dared get in the way. Me, for one.

I could feel the cuts like notches on Tom Horn's gun, working their way up and down my legs. Two blocks past what I assumed was Broadway, the cuts started screaming at me from a new source of pain: the water was turning salty. That meant the Gulf was rising with the storm surge, adding a billion gallons to the rain that whipped horizontally across the island.

As the water rose to knee-deep the walking became much harder. Trying to decide whether to high step or just trudge through, I alternated.

A monument – Civil War dead I guessed – rose out above the saltwater pond that splayed now in all directions. It stood firm even as buildings crumbled. A solitary figure sat exhausted at its base, the water around his ankles. He was leaning back against the wind, a firm jutting jaw belying his condition. Beside him, shivering and soaked, sat two dogs and a tabby cat, marooned together on this island whether they wanted to be or not.

I hailed the man who offered a half-wave in response. I came closer. "Can I help you?" I called against the noisy background of the hurricane. He shook his head.

"Nein, but I tank you very much," he curled the r in a rich German accent.

I offered my hand in some kind of recognition of our common plight. "Cale Lincoln, sir," I said, nearly shouted.

"Behrman," he answered, tipping at a hat that was long since gone. "George Augustus Behrman. I vill find my family soon," he explained. "My son Robert is taking care of them, I am sure." I nodded. The monument said *Texas Heroes*. Here was one. I waved a good-bye as a small crippled pony appeared at the granite oasis. Move on.

After an hour or more of struggling into the wind, I decided to turn right and make my way to a small neighborhood of houses I had spotted through the rain. They looked small and hopelessly positioned for destruction. If there were any people in them, they had to be taken out. I fell several times, brushing against every sort of mysterious bulk beneath the surface of the street's rivermuck. Three times what I grabbed was soft, pliable. Three times I pulled the thing to the surface. Three more bodies, all stripped naked by the surging waters, limbs in carefree abandon and oddly cantered. The first one I pulled up over my shoulder and carried up to a drier surface; the others I let sink back into their unchosen grave.

When I reached the first house, I clambered up steps on hands and knees, pushed the front door open and shouted inside. No answer. No echo. A door somewhere farther in the house slammed open and shut, keeping some death rhythm that I wasn't interested in. I left.

The second house had no front door, had no front wall, for that matter. Just the shell, most of the roof cantilevered over for viewing from the sidewalk, water and sand swirling through the living room. Living room. I saw two boots lying in a doorway, to the kitchen it turned out. They had not been left behind by their owner. He had been left behind by the killing storm.

The third house, a large two-story with columns and in fair shape, was jammed with people.

I banged on the door until a woman creaked it open. She was disheveled from head to ankle, sopping wet, her blouse torn off at one shoulder. Her eyes were wide. A gust of wind struck me in the back and hurled me against the door. It smashed against her wrist and threw her off balance backward into the crowded room. I let myself in.

Pushed against the door until the latch caught. The windows on either side vibrated in a minor key. It was dark in the house. My eyes finally focused, and I looked into a swarm of people deathly afraid. They huddled together, I rough counted twenty-five or so, clutching each other for a comfort no one could muster. There were children, and an infant cuddled in a man's arms, swaddling clothed. It made no sound.

"My name's Cale Lincoln," I said for no particular reason except that it was true. "Is there someone here in charge?" I asked as an afterthought. What difference it made.

Eyes cast about furtively. The woman I had nearly knocked to the floor absentmindedly brushed the folds in her soaked skirt, looked right at me. "I'm Mrs. Ketchum. This is my home." She raised one arm in a simple gesture. "These are my neighbors."

"Ma'am," I nodded, and walked right up to her, close to her face. "We need to get these folks to higher ground," I whispered.

She looked at me blankly. "Where will we go?"

"I don't know, ma'am. Towards town. Higher ground," I repeated.

"My husband isn't here," she explained. "He went out earlier this morning, over to Unger's Grocery. When he returns, we'll see." She set her jaw.

"Where's the grocery?" I asked.

"At Q and 41st." She sort of pointed across the house to her right.

"Where are we now?" I had no idea.

"On 33rd," she said. "N Street is there." She pointed again.

"Well, Mrs. Ketchum," I ventured my argument again after a moment of thinking up nothing else, "the water is better up across Broadway. I've just come from there. The buildings are in pretty good shape. It's six blocks and with the wind at your back. I think everyone could get there all right." I looked over her shoulder at the others. Maybe.

"I'll help you," I added.

Mrs. Ketchum turned her head to stare back into the huddled masses. No one spoke. No one even moved. They were frozen in terror. The constant noise of the wind and rain had turned them to stone. She turned back to me.

"Thank you, Mr. Lincoln," she said in such a polite, genteel voice that for an instant we were at tea in the parlor. "We will wait for Mr. Ketchum."

"But Ma'am," I started -

"Thank you, sir," she raised one hand to me. She stepped back, closer to them than me. "Mr. Ketchum will return directly."

That was the end of it. For emphasis, the hurricane blew the front door open at that moment with a great crashing noise. It swung in and around to the wall, slamming a crack along the pasteboard. I jumped with the sudden sound, and a congregant gasp went up from the huddle of people. The rain, coursing sideways through the doorway, pelted me in the back of my neck like gravel. Mrs. Ketchum instinctively spread her arms out as if to protect her inherited house guests.

No more reason to stay. I grappled the door closed as I backed out onto the porch, and heard a shuffle of furniture being thrown against it inside.

The water in the street had risen another foot in the few moments I had been away. It was racing up 33rd from the beach, speckled with lumber and masonry and wire, an ugly brown that hid whatever floated below. Whoever.

I saw the wagon as I stepped into the swirl. It was still a hundred yards away from me, and I could barely make out the figures surrounding it. It was moving across the island, on O

Street, I guessed correctly. The storm surge was up above its ragged wheels, and it was moments from being mired down. Its one horse was working hard but in vain.

I fought the wind and the rain, bending far over to make myself a smaller target, my face almost in the water. It took me fifteen minutes to make the half block, glancing up every so often to see if the wagon was real, was still there. It had stopped by the time I reached it.

Two nuns sat in the buckboard seat, both badly beaten by the storm. One held the reins, the other had one arm wrapped around the first, her free hand gripping the edge of the seat to keep both of them up there. Their horse had its ears flat against its head. His face turned in my direction as I arrived. The sisters didn't notice me at first. I patted the horse on its neck, and looked up to catch the riders' attention. When they did, I half waved to them. Started to shout. Futile gesture. Made my away down the horse's side, reached up for the seat and pulled myself up until I was poorly balanced off the ground but not quite in the wagon. The nun on the left nearest me bent over until her mouth was at my ear.

"Could you help us, please?" she shouted at the top of her voice while still sounding civil. "We need to get back to the children." I glanced past her and into the wagon bed. There were five crates and two small barrels nestled together, three or four inches of sand and water pooling around.

"Where are the children?" I shouted back. Probably didn't sound as civil. She pointed generally behind her, up the island away from town. They had been heading away from their destination. Maybe the storm gave them no choice. "How many?"

"Ninety-three," she answered immediately. "At the orphanage."

Damn. I didn't say that to her.

The storm took on a new strength suddenly, lifting me off the wagon and launching me into the thick air. As I fell, I saw the buckboard raise up on its side, tearing the axle away and tossing crates, barrels, and the two sisters in my direction. I landed unceremoniously in the saltwater stream, catching myself from being swept away by slamming my feet to the ground somewhere beneath the waves. I regained some balance and looked in the direction of the wagon.

It lay on its side, its bed opened at me. Both barrels and all but one of the crates long gone already. The horse, reined only to the broken axle piece, had turned away from the wind and stood stock still. The nuns had disappeared in an instant.

I looked around into the whirlpool, went crazy. Threw myself into the muck over and over again, reaching out in every direction. I shouted sounds against the storm's energy, slammed my open hands on the surface a hundred times. Cuts appeared on every finger, palms, wrists and up to my elbows. I pulled up boards and rocks and weeds, heaving them away from where I splashed about. I searched for three minutes. Seemed like days. Exhausted, I walked forward and collapsed into the wagon bed lean-to, braced against the wind.

"Come on, Caleb," Momma said gently. "We'll be all right now. It will be all right." Her voice was reassuring to this seven year old. I took her outstretched hand and looked toward the front doors of the church where we had been hiding. Behind us, the priest stood beside the dark wood altar rail, one hand leaning on it. He had white hair, I remember, pulled straight back. And his white collar. Everything else about him was black, shirt and suit and shoes. I don't know why I noticed. It was a moment so clear.

Momma had been talking to him for a long while, at least in child's time. We had snuck into the church the night before, after skipping through alleyways and backyards in the darkness. The dogs that had first come at us at the boardinghouse still wailed behind us, a block or so lead was all we managed.

The little Maryland church stood at the end of the town, with only the crooked road beyond it, and orchards. The door was open and we hurried in. We scrambled up to the front of the chancel, Momma paused to kneel and make the sign. I didn't.

Hours went by. The dogs stopped barking in the distance. First light announced itself with a glimmer through the stained glass. The side door

*opened and he came in. Saw us. Didn't react. Walked to us. Momma bent
down on a knee, but he reached for her elbows and pulled her to her feet.
I stood a step away, looking at the floor.*

*They talked in a whisper for some time. I didn't move. The priest kept
nodding his head, as if he understood and knew what to do. He pointed
several times outside, as if giving directions. "Four miles," I heard him say.
"It will be all right when you get there," he told her. He looked over at me
then, and smiled. "It will be all right, son," his voice was convincing. "No
one will harm you there."*

*Momma and I walked down the aisle to the double doors. I looked
back again at the priest, who nodded at me. Momma looked forward.*

*Opened the door and stepped out into the pre-dawn gray. A horse
whinnied in surprise. The torches threw a flickering yellow light against
the wall of the church building. One of the white hooded figures pointed
at Momma -*

I shook off the nightmare. Looked around at the nightmare
I had to deal with this time. The hurricane was taking a breath,
the wind subsiding to a duller roar. The rain fell in a more verti-
cal path, the river around me hadn't let up.

I was braced against the inverted wagon bed, water up to
my knees. I looked back toward Galveston, from whence I had
struggled for the last several hours. It was a bleak picture. Ruined
houses as far as I could see, with only one or two standing erect
as if they had no interest in being damaged like their neighbors.

Piles of debris everywhere, mostly under water. Like icebergs I had seen when I'd gone to the Klondike. So much mystery not seen, below the surface.

The old gelding blocked my view when he stepped in front of where I leaned. Seeking shelter, thinking I had come up with a good solution. He looked at me. I thought he would say something like "what the hell are we doing here?" He just stared.

I took the reins and halter off him, loosed the axlerod and ignored it as it sunk. I had already decided what we would do next.

I had no clear idea where that orphanage was, but the general direction I could guess. I'd never make it walking. A boat could've floated by and not surprised me. But I didn't see one at the moment. The wagon was busted all to hell. My friend and I were headed to find the children.

I took the moment to speak quietly to my mount. The storm obliterated every word, but I guessed it didn't matter to the horse. I figured he didn't want to ride back down the island, but he didn't want to be left alone either. I eased up on his back. He shook his head furiously. I pulled at his mane and he turned for me. I nudged his ribs and we started down O Street. There was an orphanage out there somewhere.

We made two blocks in thirty minutes, and not a living soul. To my left, into the howl, the island was being stripped bare.

Ahead of me and off to my right were piles of what had been houses and beach buildings, fences and landscaping, people.

On the third block heading west, I saw three men walking at me, bent against the storm. They held on to each other's arms and coats, looking down, moving forward. The lead fellow nearly walked into me where I had held up my ride. He jumped, startled, looked up at me. "H'lo," he shouted. I gave a bleak wave with one hand. "Where you headed?" he inquired.

"Orphanage," I shouted back. He looked back at the other two men and said something to them. They shook their heads in tandem.

"Can't go there," he yelled at me. "Too dangerous. Water's up." He made a motion with his arms at his chest.

"Have to," I said back. Firm. We stared at each other.

"Head to the beach," he said after a moment, pointing. "Men at the battery will help you get there. Call for Cap'n Rafferty."

"Could use some help," I suggested.

"Can't. Gotta get to town. Work to do there." He waved a goodbye in my direction. "What's your name?" he hollered as he stepped aside.

"Lincoln," I shouted.

"Ketchum," he said back. "Chief of police," he added. I looked straight into his eyes.

"Just come from your house," I said. "Wife's fine. Folks need to get outa there."

"Thanks. They'll be fine. House'll stand." He turned to the other two, shrugged a shoulder in command, walked on. Neither of them looked up at me. See ya.

I nudged my new best friend in his haunches, and we started down 45th Street, headed for the beach and right into the teeth of the hurricane.

It was probably nearing 2:00, maybe later. I had lost any accounting after my talk with Cline. The sun was elsewhere on the planet, darkness protruding from the skies. After five hundred yards of struggling upstream, I dismounted, grabbed the horse with a fistful of mane, and we tugged forward. Neither of us wanted to be here.

I spotted the beach. It had lost its distinction with the island around me. Water was knee deep, sand the same. The quagmire spiraled in every direction, making strange kaleidoscope designs of which I cared not one damn. Driftwood - from Cuba for I all I knew - piled everywhere. The piles rocked in the wind, limbs and pieces flying off the buttresses as afterthoughts, whistling through the air. It would be only hours later when whistling things became deadly.

We moved generally to our right now, the howling striking my left side like pin pricks. Fort Crockett lay tattered and nearly unrecognizable as anything manmade. It had not defended the island against this enemy. Massacre came to mind. No buildings were left standing. Several foundations reared up from the muck. Plank walls swam around without intentions. The noise deafened with no ears to hear. The surf crashed in browns and grays and white foam that quivered. The foam glowed in the dark.

In the center of where the fort had apparently stood once upon a time, a steel bunker held its position like the old mission's chapel in San Antonio. I had stood in that chapel just two years earlier.

"Men," TR hollered in his high-pitched voice. His toothy grin flashed across a hundred faces like a burst of sunlight. "We are headed for a moment of greatness soon," he began shrilly. "Our flag goes before us with the strength of a thousand brave souls, and we follow with pride. Unlike the brave ones who fell at this place sixty years ago," he paused for typically dramatic effect, "we shall overwhelm our enemy, the enemy of liberty, the enemy of democracy, the enemy of those who fight for peace and prosperity in this Western Hemisphere." A hurrah went up from the Rough Riders. Several fired their pistols into the dusty Texas air.

"We may not all return," he cautioned. He adjusted his pince nez out of habit, waved both arms into the air. "But we shall do our duty in the name of our Constitution and our place in a world that has called upon us. We

shall stand strong, ride hard, and fight our way to victory! To Victory!" I
shouted with the rest of them.

"Rafferty!" I shouted, pounding my fist against the hull of the
bunker. If he was alive and still on the island, it would have to be
inside this steel container. I looked about and picked up a shattered two by four as it drifted by. Swung it against the wall until
it disintegrated. The echo inside the chamber must have been
horrible, but I needed Rafferty and his men if I was gonna do any
good at the orphanage. Or find it.

A knock finally answered mine. I could barely make it out in
the storm, my ear pressed against the bunker. Another sound. It
moved to the back of the unit, inching its way as if guiding me.
I followed, grappling my way to the rear, away from the beach,
until I found the steel hatch. More sounds. I pounded twice on
the door. Movement. A crack as it opened. Then stopped.

I pursed my lips at the crack and shouted into it. Turned my
head to listen.

"We can let you in," said a voice from within.

"I need you out here," replied at the top of my lungs. I stepped
back so the door could swing open.

It pulled shut. The crack disappeared. I banged on the door.
No reply. Again. Nothing. I lost my balance as a shift of wind hit
me with a right cross, stepped backwards and slammed into the

horse. I had completely forgotten about him, figuring he'd be gone by now. At least he was with me.

Couldn't blame the ones in the bunker.

I lifted myself on to the horse's back, gained some balance, wrapped my arms around his neck and urged him forward. He stepped gingerly over some debris, shook his head, kept on.

The orphanage, or what was left of it, rose up through the darkness and wet a half hour — but probably not a mile - after we left the fort grounds. Most of its roof was gone, and one wall was battered like a ram had pummeled it during the siege. All the windows were busted out, ragged pieces of curtain flailing out the north side openings, calling for help that wasn't coming. Present company excluded.

The water covered almost all of the first floor, a torrent of mush swirling through from one side and ejaculating out the other, angrier still. One opening threw a spray of the muck like a fire hose.

I slid off the horse and into waist deep crud, paddling with my arms and taking long, high steps the last fifty yards. Piles of wood and concrete had jammed against the building, and I scrambled up the temporary embankment until I could grab a splintered sill. I peered inside the gloom. The wind shrieked as it hit the edifice, a terrible scream of anguish that echoed through the emptied rooms of the orphanage. I screamed with it, but the storm's noise buried mine. Water puddled for as far inside as I could see. The furniture was gone, wiped away or slung halfway to Houston. One bureau had smashed itself against a wall. Only one drawer remained, half open and crooked. A sock dangled from a splinter it stuck on, alternately waving its distress signal then falling back limp. Where was its owner, I wondered, knowing the answer.

I managed my way around the corner of the building, still picking along the ten foot pile of gathered detritus. Another empty window socket, and a third.

As I gripped the edge of the next window, a small hand reached around and grabbed my wrist. I was so startled I nearly fell into the whirlpool below. Held on. Both hands on the sill. Swung a leg inside, let the momentum tumble me inside. Hit the wet floor hard, legs akimbo. Came up on my hands and knees. Two bare feet stood in front of me, inches away. They were connected to two slender legs, which disappeared up into flimsy, soaked pants. I followed the skeletal shape up to its head. A boy, teenager maybe, looked back at me. He had his hands planted firmly on his hips, elbows out. His hair was tousled, and a cut extended from his left ear down across his throat to his chest. It was still bleeding, catching up in a torn tee shirt. He was smiling as he extended one hand.

"Help you up, Mister," he said in a strong voice. I fell back on my haunches, looked at him full view for a moment, accepted his invitation.

"Thanks," I mumbled, standing. I was nearly twice as tall as my rescuer, but he seemed somehow plenty big enough for the occasion. Maybe it was the way he stood. Defiant, confident. And what the hell was there to be confident about?

"Will Murney," he introduced himself, shaking my hand.

"Pleased to meet you, Will Murney," I acknowledged. "Cale Lincoln." He nodded.

"Where'd you come from?" he asked, looking just past me out the severed window. "You bring help?"

I shook my head. "Just me." He made a funny look. "'K," he said. "C'mon."

He turned and walked through the battered doorway, out into a hall. I followed him across the building. Water stood everywhere. The wind was roaring. He stopped outside the only shut door we had passed. Knocked hard. Pushed it open at the same time. I followed him in.

The room, maybe a dining hall, large, was filled with kids. All ages, maybe from four or five up. Seventy, eighty or more. As my eyes got used to the inner darkness, I saw the nuns. Maybe eight. No one spoke. No one was crying. Silent against the storm. Will Murney strode across the room, spoke to one of the sisters, pointed at me twice. She shook her – head. He returned to my side.

"They're going. Gonna walk up the island," he explained matter of factly.

"No. They need to stay here," I replied after a moment thinking about it. "Too dangerous out there. They'll never make it." I looked up and around me, then back at Will. "Building should hold. Mebbe not. Still better than heading out."

"It's what I told Sister," Will agreed. "She said 'God would provide.'"

"Well, I can't argue that one way or another," I said gently. "But I've been out there all day. God may be at work somewhere else than Galveston Island right now." I didn't usually worry a lot about my theology.

That's when I noticed the ropes. Each of the nuns stood at the head of a line of nine or ten children. A clothesline rope had been knotted around her waist, then drawn along the children, wrapped once around each of their waists to the last child. They were lined up in orderly rows, preparing to walk out into this hell, tied together for safety.

Or death.

"Will," I said so only he could hear, "we have to keep these folks here."

I don't think I ever actually said the last words, was just thinking them when hell burst inside the orphanage.

The storm struck its lethal blow like dynamite taking out the side of a mountain in Colorado. There was a single squeaking sound as the whole building trembled once, then caved in on itself. Someone screamed. Everyone looked up at the same time. The ceiling bent against the pressure, deformed, and crinkled like a folding map. The wall off to my left erupted in an explosion of board and paper and nails. The ceiling crumpled in a hundred pieces, showering the dining hall and its prisoners with deadly projectiles. The last thing I remember seeing was a huge support beam cracking in half above me, holding its breath before it plunged at my head.

I grabbed the boy by his elbow and launched the two of us sideways, hurling us both out into the hallway. It was holding for the moment off to our left. We scrambled to our feet, running and crawling to the slim opening ahead. Without a pause we dove out the window. The wind caught us mid-air and propelled us away from the collapsing building. I couldn't look back as I flew and fell, only heard the murderous sound of the orphanage evaporating in the deluge.

3

Will and I hit the pile of debris faces first, caught some projecting plank, held on to it and each other. Just held on. The storm surge struck us over and over. Ten minutes. Ten days? Salty water ran up over our outstretched bodies, attacking at each cut and scrape like a devilish surgeon's scalpel. We kept our eyes shut tight most of the time to keep the salt spray out. I peeked at Will every few moments. He lay stoic. His shirt had ripped away, his pants legs shredded.

I kept one arm thrown over his back. The other wrapped around a post.

The storm held its breath. We scrambled off the pile and jammed ourselves against the north wall of what had been the orphanage. For the first time we looked at the damage. The second floor of the building had vanished into the bowels of the hurricane. Hallway, window sills, dining hall, all gone. No children, no sisters. What had been its floor now served – in pieces – as its temporary ceiling. But two of the walls had crumbled, the west wall losing its grip as we watched. Only the bricks where we sought momentary shelter held. That wouldn't last.

A shout of some primal origin echoed up from somewhere inside the wrecked building. Will pulled away from me and disappeared around the wall all in one motion. I hated to leave my little lean-to, dammit. I followed.

I spotted the teenager in the darkness of the first floor, shoulder deep in water, moving stolidly toward the scream's source. I slid into the muck to follow. The scream stopped. So did I. In a moment I saw Will coming back towards me, his arms flailed out from each side. In each fist was a mop of hair connected to what looked at first like floating heads. I reached for my companion and grabbed his belt, pulled him up against me. Backpeddled to the opening where we had entered.

In the shallower water, the two heads now displayed the bodies they were connected to. Two boys Will's age and size, looking like drowned rats, staring blankly at me. Will pressed his mouth against my collarbone.

"My pals," he shouted. "This is Albert," he raised the head on his left. "The other's Francis." I nodded.

Pulled myself up out of the darkness, Will with me. He never let go the boys' hair, dragged them outside with us. The storm still held its breath, catching a moment before blasting the island again. A huge tree, maybe fifty feet tall earlier that day, drifted by the brick wall. Headed for town, I supposed. The tree seemed impossibly light enough to bob high above the debris. Without a moment to decide otherwise, I lifted Will onto the back of the tree. He didn't resist. Pulled his two friends up with them. Strong branches became foot and hand holds for the trio.

Before he was whisked away, I hoped to safety, I grabbed him by the back of his neck, pulled my face into his, and smiled. "Will Murney, you're gonna be all right. You take care of your friends. I'll see you in town tonight." Wishful thinking. He smiled back, turned back toward the trunk and buried himself against it. Drifted away.

I watched from my disintegrating outpost until they vanished in the darkness. There was no more reason to stay at this place. Going back to town seemed implausible, but staying out on this part of the island more so. I looked around wistfully, thinking my sturdy mount might show up once more.

I began to walk, north and east. There were no streets or blocks left here, only piles of what had been this end of the city. Body parts threw themselves out from below the stacks of driftwood, as if reaching for a safety no longer available. Arms outstretched in one last failed effort for rescue. Legs bared and shoeless pointing in every direction except to life.

The storm reached out and lashed me once again, the respite over. Walking with the wind this time made the voyage barely easier, as I stumbled and fell repeatedly. I walked without meaning, bent and like the dead who surrounded me. I looked but didn't see; listened but there was nothing to be heard. Screeches startled me several times, as houses leaned over and then fell into the swirl. Glass cut at my legs, unknown things stubbed at my feet. I dripped sweat and saltwater and blood in a concoction not fit for snake oil.

And I just kept on. Stopping seemed incongruous. It would feel so good just to give up, lie down and let the storm unite me with a thousand residents. But what a waste of my day to end it now. And I kept thinking of Will Murney. I expected him to make it: I had to see that through.

I walked for two eternities, or maybe an hour. The water began to recede ahead of me, though the storm hadn't abated. I was approaching the high level of the island, headed back toward town. Or where town had been that morning. The walking came more easily, just knee deep mostly.

The most insane thing I might have seen next I saw. A boat making its way down a street from my left. And not adrift.

I half waved and hurried my stumbling steps, meeting up with the rescue vessel as it started across my path. A man in a heavy jacket and leather helmet knelt near the front of the boat, an oar in his hands. He looked straight ahead, didn't see me until I had struck the side of his vessel with my fist. He jumped, turned to look at me.

Behind him, huddled together and partially under a thick black tarp, were bodies. Seven, eight. They hardly moved. Without invitation nor introduction, I curled over the side and fell to the bottom on my back. The rowing man turned back to face forward, calling casually over his shoulder.

"Brophey's the name, friend." He took up his rowing. I couldn't even respond. I closed my eyes, wrapped one arm over my face, crooked my knees and turned over on one side. The rain beat down. I was unconscious in seconds.

I had fashioned a hammock from some ragged netting stored below, strung it up on the starboard deck, and now swung gently in the Caribbean breeze. The ship rocked me in and out of a fitful sleep. I had a sense of fellow sailors wandering about close by, but didn't care. Days on this tub since we'd left the states. Squalls bringing breakfast back up, night skies of a million galaxies. Our sister ship had capsized two days out of port, sending the horses to a watery grave. The 1ˢᵗ Cavalry afoot in the hills of

Cuba: what a ridiculous picture that would be. Mebbe Mr. Hearst would call us the Rough Runners instead.

My nap was interrupted by the grumbling of my commander as he stalked by. TR had been pacing the deck since the moment we had left, slapping his hand against his side interminably, adjusting his glasses, staring out across the sea. News of the Oregon's arrival had only barely tempered his general disgust at our situation. "Goddamn the French," he repeated hourly, as if that would shame their ghosts into finishing the Nicaragua passage. "We could've done it," he emphasized. "Goddamn we could've done it."

"Land ho," cried the lookout, playing Columbus for everyone's benefit. "Santiago," he rhymed and pointed. We all looked in spite of ourselves.

We'd been plying the island coast for hours, peering at it off to our right as we steamed around the eastern point. Santiago Bay was our destination, a jungle full of unknown dangers our target. Two or three of the Easterners, poets they called themselves thinking it was a title, seemed nervous during the trip. I opened one eye at the hail and happened to catch one of them in my sight. He gulped in an exaggerated style, and turned away from the side. I made a note: steer clear of that one when the battle begins.

I closed my eye again, to steal one last cache of sleep before the activity began. Ten feet away I could hear the slap of TR's hand against his side. It had a different ring to it, I thought at the time. Excitement now, no more frustration. The Oregon was ready, so were we. This was what *we'd gone to San Antone for, this is why we had signed up. The fight was on. Bring it on. And goddamn the French, just for good measure.*

"Mister," someone shook me gently. What a peculiar voice for a sailor, I mused in my stupor. "Mister," the voice whispered again. I squinted. What the hell -

If I had died in the storm, the most exquisite angel in Heaven had been assigned my pitiful soul. Thank you, God, wherever You are.

She stared down at me, soft black hair brushing my face. I lay flat on my back. I could feel my arms splayed out from my sides, hanging over the cot. My feet strayed well past the end of the bed. I opened my eyes another notch. Stared into those deep brown eyes, flashed some distant memory of a poem about pools, tried to smile. The crease hurt my face, so I stopped. My arms weighed just under a thousand pounds, and wouldn't respond to first instructions. Impossibly tired, I just lay still and stared.

"Hello," she said in honeyed language. Soft. "You are safe now," she continued, picking her words carefully. "You've been unconscious for some time, but the doctor says you will be all right." I hadn't thought to ask. I mumbled something in response. It made no sense. She smiled at my feeble attempt, blinked, touched my face with her right hand. "It will be all right," she repeated. "Lie still."

I didn't mind lying still for the next millenium, on condition she would not move out of my sight. In a recess of my soaked brain came the thought, Please keep your hand on my face forever. I was pretty sure those words didn't make it any further. Damn.

"Can you tell me your name," she asked after a pause. When I couldn't she offered hers. "My name is Abigail." As in the most beautiful name in the annals of history, I believed in that moment.

With whatever reserves were left I managed to lift my head from the cot until I was only inches from her face. "Dinner tonight?" I stuttered.

Abigail the Angel frowned - it made her even more beautiful - and then smiled a full smile, not having moved her face a millimeter away. Her laugh was the medicine of the ages. "Come for me at eight," she replied.

And me without a thing to wear.

My head fell back to the cot. I closed my eyes for several minutes, awake and trying to conjure up some strength from deep inside. It finally came. I pulled up on my elbows and glanced around. The angel was still there, sitting in a stiff-backed chair beside me. She wore a navy blue dress with a white lace collar. No jewelry, nothing to tie her hair, her sleeves rolled up to her elbows. The dress was torn at each shoulder seam, and another across her waist. Patches of stains dotted the front. Blood? Her hair was unmanaged, a curl swinging down on her forehead. She rivaled the czar's wife in elegance. And she was still smiling at me. At me.

"Cale," I announced in a far away voice.

She leaned forward. "A pleasure, Cale," she said simply. Sat back.

"Where am I?"

"St. Mary's Infirmary," she answered. "On the east end of the island. Mr. Brophey brought you and the others here in his boat," she explained. "He's been rescuing people for hours. Young Mr. Harris came with you," she nodded her head just past where I lay. I turned my head. A young boy maybe seven was asleep in the cot next me, curled up tight under a thick olive green blanket. "James Woods Harris," she introduced me. "All of his family is missing still." The angel's voice cracked at the end of the sentence.

"Will Murney?" I managed weakly. She put her hands in her lap, one on top of the other. Genteel. Stared across the wide, busy room. Thought a moment. Frowned. Stopped frowning. "No," she said. "I don't know." He was all right, I knew that somehow.

The boy next to me coughed in his sleep. We both looked at him. Abigail leaned forward. "Cale, you need to rest now. Mr. Brophey said you'd been wading out on the west end when he found you. Out from the orphanage." The last sentence ended in something like a question. I looked hard into her eyes. Shook my head slowly. She understood, bit her lip in anguish, sat back.

I sat up. She reached over and placed her hand against my chest. I noticed that my shirt and coat were gone. Her touch was firm, but I needed to move. I put my hand on hers, to keep it against my chest, and swung my leaden legs around as I sat up. I thought perhaps I could keep her hand there until the world came to an end. It was worth a try.

She pulled her hand away, demurely but not to object. Both hands on her hips, elbows out as she sat up straight. "You mustn't move," she insisted. "The doctor has bandaged your injuries, but there may be broken bones as well." I did a quick mental inventory. Everything hurt. Maybe every bone was broken. A rib or two, I felt for sure. My left ankle throbbed now as I thought about it. The rest was just soreness. I'd been there many times before.

"The storm?" I started.

"Still strong," she answered the longer question that was in there. "It's nearly dusk, but it's been dark for hours. Damage reports are coming in to the infirmary with the survivors. I can't believe how terrible it must be out there." I was a believer. In angels and hurricanes.

"Are you in charge?" I asked. She shook her head, pointed across the room. I followed her direction, saw a tall, broad-shouldered man bent over a table filled with medicine bottles and gauze. He was nearly as big as me, I estimated. He wore a brown top coat, even though it seemed hot inside to me.

"Mr. Scott," she informed me. "He's coordinated the efforts here since I arrived. I came with others from the Tremont this afternoon." I stared at her, dumbstruck. Her eyes widened at my expression. I wanted to say, Are you telling me that you were at the hotel all along and I didn't know it? Am I the dumbest, blindest man in Galveston?

"I need to speak to him," I said instead. I made as if I were going to stand up. The rest of my body thought that was humorous, and didn't budge. I took a deep breath that hurt, summoned some reserves, and tried it again. I made it off the cot and lost my balance, heading for the floor. My angel caught me in her arms. Nothing genteel about that grasp. Firm and strong and sure. I stumbled to my feet as she held me, put my hands on her upper arms below the shoulder, and gained my balance.

I stood a full head taller than her. We could freeze in this position, I thought, and just pass eternity as statues in an embrace. It was tempting.

"Thank you, Abbie," I said, my voice improving. "I have to get back out there," I tried to explain. She stared back at me, right between my eyes with gun barrel intensity. Started to object. I squeezed her arms. Her shoulders sagged an inch. No use protesting.

"Will you be careful," it was a statement more than a query.

I looked as deep inside of her as I could. "We have a dinner date, don't we?"

I pulled her to me without thinking, kissed her lightly on the forehead curl, turned and walked across the room. Longest walk of my life, I decided on the way.

I reached the medicine table where the man in charge continued to work. He turned as I came up to him, extended his hand which I took firmly.

"Scott," he said in a strong bass voice. "Zachary Scott."

"Cale Lincoln, Doc."

He shook his head. "Not a doctor. Just helping out where I can." I nodded. No need for titles or licenses right now.

"What's the word coming in, Doc," I asked, ignoring his non-credentials. "How can I help out there?"

"Lucas Terrace just caved in," he began. "Someone just said. Might be survivors still there." I shrugged for directions. "Oh. Due south of here. Six blocks?"

"Okay. Thanks." I shook his hand again, started for the door. Stopped. He looked up at me. "Doc, if a boy comes in here named Will Murney, about fourteen mebbe, tell him I said h'lo and that I'll see him." Scott registered the request, nodded. Waved a hand of farewell in my direction. Went back to work. I glanced past him. Abbie was sitting beside the boy's cot, her hand on his shoulder. She looked in my direction. A half smile.

I went out the door into the storm. I would see that face again, by God, I swore.

4

It was 6:30. Outside just seemed like sundown, which, if the sun still existed somewhere in the universe, might be another two hours away. The darkness had taken control of the island around 2:00, about the time I was putting Will Murney and his two collaborators on that motoring tree. The wind had shifted, I noticed, probably more than once since I'd knocked out. I knew only enough about hurricanes to be dangerous to others who might ask: something about low pressure, winds counter-clockwise, stronger on the east and nor'east side. This one was packing enough for the island, that I decided we had gotten the worst part it had to offer. The eye must've been down the coast a few miles. Lucky them.

Now the wind was blowing from the north, but swirling so desperately as to confuse even a real weatherman, which I was not. I was walking along Mechanic Street, having lost my bearings the moment I stepped out of the infirmary. It was the highest point on the island, someone had said, but there was water and its debris everywhere. The water had crisscrossed the city, maybe more than once. The winds had blown the Gulf up first and then back. The bay had then made its bid to control the nearby business district - the Strand they call it - and nearly did. Now both contenders waded in, literally.

The wind howled. Furious at something. Vengeance came to mind. Don't know what these folks had done to deserve it, though. But then I hadn't been on the island but a couple of weeks.

Just as I came up to a two-story building where a crinkled sign said Ritter's Café was to be found, two things happened, nearly in the same instant.

In the first instant the wind suddenly increased its velocity as if someone had flung the barn door open. From a million miles an hour to two, I guessed inexactly. The whole city block where I stood trembled, like an earthquake had joined the ruckus.

And in the second instant the water level came up, a foot, two feet, just in the time it took to think that. I was no seafarer, though I'd had plenty of days out there, but I guessed what had happened. It wasn't the rain, it wasn't the water that had gathered from the storm.

It was the sea herself.

She had just covered the island in that moment. Like the island had suddenly sunk two feet. Isaac told me later it was what they were calling a storm surge, the wind and pressure literally lifting the ocean - the Gulf - in the blink of an eye. No tidal wave, no crashing breakers. It wasn't there, and then it was. Just like that.

I heard two sounds in the next sixty seconds, neither of which I much cared for. The first sound was the bats. A half million of them had responded to the increased wind and were coming from every orifice the city had. Black and brown and sleek and sure of themselves, whipping through the air at blinding speeds, spiraling, turning and twisting, and all the while, the screeching. They slammed into and through plate glass windows, busted streetlights all to hell, the exploding glass propelled like New Orleans fireworks into the inky sky. One of the creatures whooshed by my left ear, not missing it by a hair. I leaned instinctively away as it flew on. I watched in some stupored fascination as the bats angled their way through the streets and alleyways.

Several people made a dash across Mechanic Street just ahead of me, maybe a hundred feet or so. Their heads bent into the howl, hands up to shade their faces against the prickly rain that pelted them. The bats seemed to target them as one black cloud. The leaders dove from the sky and raked the runners. Three of them, two skirted and I presumed were women, stopped in their tracks, mid-stride. There was the briefest pause as if they were playing the children's game of freeze tag. Then their arms went limp to their sides.

And three severed heads rolled off slumping shoulders, splashing into the street's stream. The lifeless bodies followed without resistance and disappeared into the swirl.

Those weren't bats that did that. A screeching projectile missed me - again - and careened into the wall where I stood watching the tragic drama unfold. I grabbed for it as it slid down the bricks, thinking to wring its neck in frustration over what I'd just witnessed. It did not try to wriggle away, did not fight me. It was a slate shingle. There had been no bats at all. More deadly still, the Galveston rooftops were yielding a weapon of mass destruction to the hurricane winds, and the shingles were slicing everything - and everyone - in their path. And only an instant of noise as a warning. No warning at all.

I pitched myself into the doorway of the building where I had been standing. Ritter's Café, I assumed. The sign was gone now, on its way to Corpus Christi, I supposed. It was dark inside, but I could hear the buzz and some laughter of a dozen men, even though my eyes refused to adjust to the shadows where they were hidden.

That's when I heard the second sound. It was a loud creak, with a timber-cracking antiphony to go with it. The sound and its echo were so distinctive, so terrible, so dread-filled, that the dozen voices stopped as one to listen. Every one of us froze. The wind outside uttered one vicious growl.

And the Ritter Café ceiling caved in. Every piece of it. Altogether, disassembling as it came, dropping the entire second floor of the building with it, rumbling like an avalanche in Switzerland, and in a three-count it was over. No dust to splay from beneath. No water splashed. No sound came after, except a kind of sigh from the collapsed building.

I stood in the shell of the door, my arms outstretched, my hands driven against the sides like one by fours on a scaffold for support. There was nothing else standing. Just the doorway. Just me. Everything else was a heap. And a dozen men gone. Just like that.

I stepped back out into the driving rain, the salty bay water skimming up my pants legs and over my knees. I no longer felt the wet: I think I had been wet since I was born. The wind whipped at me, tried to knock me into the maelstrom. I pushed back at it, shoved it like it was a drunk leaning against me. I wasn't afraid of this hurricane. I was mad as hell at it.

"Momma," I shrieked in my little boy voice. A giant hand came down from within the folds of the white sheet and grappled me by my shaking shoulder. I was lifted off the ground and slung against the side

of a dapple gray horse. I stared up, the flickering light of the torches making me blink. I looked through the torn holes of the white hood, and stared back at the piercing black eyes hiding inside. I could hear my mother gasping and struggling, but I could no longer see her. Another hooded figure had her.

The horses neighed and snorted as reins struck them in a unison movement. The mob started down the street of the small Maryland town and was quickly out in the nearby woods. The firelight bounced and slithered along trees and brush, making frightening patterns of nightmare phantoms running alongside us. I was jostled until I thought my arms and head would fall off my body, never quite in the saddle, but straddled against the horse, buffeted with every gallop.

We rode for a half hour, and it seemed like all night. When the mount finally pulled up, I was dropped unceremoniously to the ground, where I rolled to a stop. My shoulder hurt like a branding iron was jammed against it. I wiped dirty tears from my face, and looked around for Momma. The hooded giants had dismounted, a few still on horseback as sentries looking out into the darkness. Momma was being dragged by her hair across the tiny glen. She had cried all of her tears, and made not a sound as they pulled her roughly over briars and gravel.

I remember only flashes of the next few moments. A torch jammed into the soft dirt by a crooked tree. A rope dangling over a grotesque limb. A voice grumbling without sense, and a shout from the hoods. A body lifted, falling —

The body lifted and fell in the swell of the sea foam in front of me. I reached for it and grabbed sopped clothes, pulled it aside and up on to a plank that had wedged itself in a broken wall. It could have been a woman. Hard to tell anymore. I left it where someone might come along and care for it. What was left of it.

I had been stumbling back to the north east, away from the Strand. In the general direction of Lucas Terrace. Several people had pointed when I shouted for help. Most of the people were just wandering around, like me. The sea's swell had done it. So suddenly. So high. Toward the Gulf, the first floor of homes and buildings were gone. Underwater. The view was horrific, odd. Only second and third floors to see. A building standing erect, and no other for five hundred yards. Where fifty had been at Noon.

What was left of Galveston seemed to be floating. Piles. Into the darkness. Nowhere bound. An occasional scream or shout, a child's whimper now and again somehow rising above all the other sounds. But no way to focus on the sound. How the hell can you rescue them when you can't find them? I was damn mad at this thing.

I had walked another mile. I had no strength left of my own. Just will. Maybe Somebody pushing me on. I never was real clear about how that worked. But I knew I needed to be at this place that Isaac had told me about earlier in the day. As the night threatened to fall now, I pushed on. The bodies were piling everywhere now, or parts of them. Gaggles of survivors occasionally popped into view, going in every direction without purpose. They all stared straight ahead. No sound. No expression. No leader. Just alive.

Off to my right, in the distance, I heard a new noise. It was a screaming of metal, but it went on and on. It wasn't something crashing. Or falling. It was moving. Like a ghost train wrenching against its rails, its brakes on, squealing, fighting, sparks and smoke thrown to the banks. It was wide and expansive and massive and never-ending, and I hated the sound with every step I took parallel to it. I clapped my hands over my ears to make it go away. Lost my balance in the gusts. Back on my feet. Keep walking. Don't stop. Don't let the bugger get you.

The wind was at its fiercest when I came in sight of what had been Lucas Terrace. Later I would read that the wind had blown Isaac's instruments all to hell, and that 120 miles per hour was the best guess of the winds around 7:00 this evening. Some ventured guesses crazily higher. At this moment I agreed with the crazy ones. The storm was mean and it meant business.

Part of the structure had collapsed, probably some hours before judging from the debris piled around and the rumor that had made the infirmary when I woke up. One part of the roof leaned into the wind, as if it had volunteered to buffet the howl for the rest of the building. It hadn't worked. Most of a third floor was gone. Huge chunks of brick and concrete and glass had been ripped out of walls and foundations, flung like wadded paper into the sea and around the neighborhood. Hardly any windows were intact except on the side where I stood, away from direct hits by the hurricane thus far. This façade seemed almost untouched by the storm.

And in those windows were the faces. I was staring up from what had been the street and was now a fast-moving stream of sand and wood and flesh, looking into the forlorn eyes of a dozen people. There were three or four at each window, staring at nothing, eyes glazed or too-wide open, one or the other. Some had their outstretched hands against the glass, palms out, not wanting to push too hard but at the same time needing to get out. Two or three of them noticed me, a pathetic figure standing below like a cat they hadn't drug inside in time. A flicker of hope passed across their faces, and I even thought I saw some eyebrows raised in expectation.

But I was no rescue team, no army of hope. Just me. Wondering what the hell I was doing there now that I had made it to my destination. Sand peppered me all the time now, the wind was filled with it. I grit my teeth against it, my collar hunched high. It didn't help: the prickly stuff found its way through my clothes, running down inside like so much sandpaper. Getting inside what was left of Lucas Terrace seemed if nothing else a brief respite. I took a step for the one door still left on its hinges.

The storm took in a massive, sucking breath in that instant. On the second floor, a man stood alone at a window. I caught a glance of him the instant the explosion went off. The hurricane inhaled, the window disintegrated, some devilish vacuum was created, and the man simply flew out into midair and blew apart. I'd never seen anything like it, even on Kettle Hill when cannon fire had taken parts of men and turned them into so much meat. He was there, above me, poised in flight, his eyes giant brown and white circles in the middle of his face, and then he evaporated. There. And gone. Mary Mother of God.

I went inside. What was left of it. The lobby was empty, a thin layer of sand and puddles on the floor. Chairs were stacked near the door: someone had at least considered barricading themselves in before going outside instead. A plant stood defiantly in the corner, unassailed by the storm and uninterested in my ragged entrance. It was dark, very dark inside.

I heard some shuffling noises and what may have been groans or whimpers coming from down a long, pitch-black hallway. I made my way by feel, hands against the sweating walls, each step another adventure into oblivion. The sounds grew louder as I inched closer. I stumbled, once, on something hard, but kept going.

When I bumped into her she jumped with a shriek and scared the living daylights out of me, too. I didn't shriek, though. I reached through the gray and gently grasped her upper arm. She was shivering enough to make my hand tremble with her. I held her firmly to allay whatever fears consumed her, and it took a minute, but it seemed to help. She stopped shivering, a little, and turned in the shadowy hall to face me. Our noses weren't six inches apart, eyes wide forcing whatever light to bear on each other.

"What's your name?" I finally broke the silence.

"Mary," she whispered, faltered, garbled. "Mary Quayle."

"My name's Cale," I replied in a voice nearly as quiet as hers. Shouting would have frightened us both. "I can help you," I added for comfort if not convincingly.

"I'm looking for my husband," she said, so delicately that I thought her words would break apart as she said them. With that, she turned away from me and started for the darkness. I increased the strength of my grip on her arm.

"Wait," I said. "Tell me where he is, and I'll go get him. I want you to stay here where it's safer. Let me walk you to the front door, and then I'll bring your husband back." She pondered that for a moment, as if it were too many instructions thrown at her at one time. Then she shook her head – it was the most I'd seen out of her so far, and pulled at my grip.

"I'll show you. Please, let me show you." The imploring in her voice was unimpeachable. I didn't let go, but I stepped beside her and, still holding on, I led her through the hall. We both led and followed each other for ten steps until we came to some stairs. She looked pleadingly up the stairwell, and then at me. *Up there*, her eyes said. I wasn't keen on going up those or any stairs, but my choices had slimmed down to none.

We managed the stairs, gingerly and in slow motion. Paused at a turn in them. Eight, nine more to the next level of the disintegrating Lucas Terrace. I stepped out into another dark hallway, looked up and down as if I could see, listened, heard nothing, helped Mary Quayle to my side. She moved her arm just enough to indicate which direction we should go. Back to the end of the building where I'd come in. After two dozen strides I could see the light coming through a window – or what had been a window, and the dull sound of the storm that had seemed far away the last few minutes began to get louder.

We walked out of the hall and into a rather large room. There had been three windows across its outside wall, but now just gaping holes greeted us visitors. I had a bad feeling, a very bad feeling. Mary Quayle walked purposefully out of my grip and to the center sill. The wind howled just inches away, and a swirl of it bounced in and around the room for a moment before going on. I walked to her side and looked out.

I was sure of where I was. I could look down and see me standing there not five minutes before, just like the man had been doing when the storm sucked him to purgatory. I did not want to look at Mary. When I did, she was staring – hard – down into the street, as if willing Mr. Quayle to appear. I did not move, did not utter a sound. A minute went by, like it was in slow-time. Then I felt Mary Quayle's hand, small and soft and sad, curl into mine. She did not take her eyes off the street. Nothing else moved. Neither one of us breathed. She knew.

Our grotesque silence was broken by a voice, not either of ours. I turned quickly away from the window. Four haggard souls stood in the doorway from the hall. One of them, an older man, was speaking. "-rescue us?" he was saying. "Can you get us to the infirmary, sir?" I guess he meant me. The others half-nodded in agreement.

"The storm is getting worse," I answered, and I felt like I was listening to myself speak from over at one side. "We should go to the lobby downstairs, and wait there. When the storm slows up a bit, I think I can get you to safety." No guarantees, I didn't say but thought.

"That will be just fine, sir," another voice interjected. "Can we go now?" Insistence is often brought on by abject fear.

"Yes. Let's head for the stairway." I motioned past them, squeezed Mary Quayle's small hand in mine, and we made our way through the group and into the front of the procession. It darkened again and we lost our depth perception in a moment. I tried to keep at a pace that all six of us could gain, but they lagged behind. I could hear their shuffling footsteps grow distant, then a cough or some sound, then they would try to catch up. This happened several times in the space of less than fifty feet. I was frustrated at the slow pace, but I made myself get past it. Concentrate. Get these people out of here.

I heard the sound I didn't want to hear as we reached the top of the stairs. The walls moaned their intentions to fall away soon, and give up to the power of the storm that pounded on them from outside. Above me I could feel more than hear the reinforcements in the ceiling giving way. Popping sounds warned me that the building was gasping its last breath. Its bones were brittle and breaking, one by one.

"Hurry," I adjured my little parade. "We must get outside." I pushed Mary Quayle to the top step and she took my hint and hurried down into the black pit of the stairwell. I turned to the four strangers and waved my hand as if to direct them after her. They stood frozen in place. The older gentleman who had spoken up first turned and looked at the others, once by one, then back at me.

"We think it will be safer up here, out of the water." He half-pointed farther down the hall, away from the stairs, away from the light we'd just left. I was, for a brief moment, speechless.

When the words came to me, they came out crisp and clear and each with its own space.

"You will all die if you do not come with me right now." I extended my right hand toward him, and all four of them shrank back as if it were a cobra. I repeated myself, word for word, just a little bit louder and firmer. Stalemate.

Mary cried as she fell the last three steps to the ground. I broke from my incredulous staring contest with these hapless victims, dashed down the stairs tumbling two or three at a time, and reached Mary as she had landed, on all fours. I swept her up into my arms in one movement and made my way towards the door with long strides that were well beyond my own capacity at that moment. But I called on something more, something else, to get us out. Besides, I had one more task to perform in that building, and – a crazier than usual thought sped through my brain – I had an eight o'clock date with a woman named Abbie whom I had never met but once in my life.

We made the front lobby in seconds, me and my precious cargo Mary Quayle. With one hand I lifted a chair from the stack and propped it against the door sill, away from the shattered glass window but within reach of the clasp. I sat Mary Quayle down in the chair, absently brushed her torn skirt into some kind of decent folds to cover her bruised legs, and knelt down in front of her, nose to nose one more time.

"I want you to stay right here, Mary Quayle," I said with a grim smile that was supposed to be reassuring and I'm sure was anything but, "until I return." I paused. She nodded. I continued, "If someone comes by to help you, you are to go with them. If the storm comes in this window," I pointed, "I want you to walk outside and hold on to the post there." I pointed once more in the general direction of what was left of a streetlight pole. "Do you understand?" She nodded, almost vigorously.

I stood up. She grabbed me at both wrists, squeezed hard. I reached over while she held me and kissed her on her forehead. "I will be right back," I declared. Promise.

I headed down the hall one more time. To the stairs. Up the stairs, three at a time. The walls moaned, louder than before. The ceiling bent, creaked, winced in pain. Reached the top. Looked both ways. Headed to the interior of Lucas Terrace. Darkness enveloped me completely. No human sounds. I shouted, just noises. No response. My pace doubled. I ran through the dark. Stumbled. Fell. Ran. Fell again. No human sounds. The building cried out in anguish. I heard a wall collapse nearby. No light. The crashing sound faded. I ran five more steps. Hit the wall where the hallway turned. Smashed into it with both hands in front of me. I could feel my left wrist as it cracked, crumpled inside. Hit the right side of my head. Hard. Nothing cracked. My shoulder went next, separated, a searing pain shot through me to my toes. My body twisted automatically to soften the rest of the impact, and my back slammed to the wall. I stopped.

I was breathing hard. I couldn't feel my wrist, but my right shoulder was talking a blue streak to my brain. Its message was clear. I bent my knees and put my hands on them. Took three deep breaths. Got control. The ceiling cracked, louder this time than before. Right over where I stood.

I pulled myself upright. Turned. Touched the wall with my tenderized left hand to get my bearings. Slammed my right shoulder as hard as I could where I had struck before. The shoulder popped back into place. The pain went away. Came right back. Damn, my wrist hurt.

The hallway turned to the left, then back to the right once more and continued on. I made the two turns, but a new wall had been created where the rest of the building had come down, and I was blocked from continuing on. I backed back down the hallway, the turns, and assessed what had happened. No idea. Those four people had vanished. In a side room? Out some window? Underneath the rubble of what had been the hall? I knew I would never find out.

I was at the stairs and down them without thinking. The last hall led me to the lobby. My last time there. I crossed the lobby to the door before the thought struck: Mary Quayle was gone.

The chair was there. Empty. The door cracked open two inches. I pulled it open with an angry motion. She stood there on the sidewalk. Hands on her hips.

5

"Abbie!"

"Cale?" The most beautiful woman on the planet threw her hands to her face in shock. I was just thrilled she recognized me. Maybe there was a god. "Is that you?" She took a halting step in my direction, like I was some soggy apparition, a mirage in the storm that would fade if she got any closer. But her next steps were firm and bold, right into my arms. I winced as I pulled her against my chest. My broken wrist and popped shoulder seemed uninterested in my reacquaintance with this angel. She stepped back.

"You're hurt," she said simply. Several responses, most sarcastic, came to mind. "No," I lied. Odd choice. She was looking me over, anxious, like she didn't believe me. Hm. She placed one hand gently against my chest, her other touching my arms, chin, and coming to rest on the left side of my face. And those eyes boring into mine. Then she wrapped her arms around me just above my waist and we stood there like that. Hoping that the gods would freeze us as a statue forever symbolizing human love, I was deeply disappointed when she pushed back again.

"Where have you been? What has happened to you? What about the people inside?" The questions tumbled out on one another before I could answer. I had no idea where to start, and wouldn't have made much of an explanation before the rest of the Lucas Terrace building collapsed behind me in one giant exhale.

Without even looking back to see what I could feel what happening, I dance-stepped Abbie and me away and into the street, covering her as much as I could from whatever might start flying from what had been a three-story structure. Bricks bounced and timber screeched as the building imploded. I glanced over my throbbing shoulder. A resilient cloud of mortar dust spewed from the collapse, into the rain and wind. Dispersed and vanished in a moment.

The only thing left standing was the doorway I had just exited, part of the lobby and one tragically empty room just above it. What was left of the third floor bent into the craggy shape of a steeply-angled roof, and nestled precariously on top of the left-over edifice like a triangular hat. Then Lucas Terrace was silent. Its last breath gone. *Morte.*

Abbie the Angel and I stood for only a few moments staring at what had been. The rain pelted us like needles, the wind had not given in an inch, and the water still rose. I had not been dry since – when would that have been, anyway? – and I needed to get the both of us to higher ground.

Without speaking I took Abbie by the hand and we started up the island, headed more or less for the Strand. I had taken three steps before she tugged at me to stop. I did.

"We have to go to the beach," she informed me. I pursed my lips to ask why but she hurried on. "It's why I was here in the first place. Mr. Scott received an urgent message for help an hour ago. There are families trapped in their homes down near the beach," she motioned absently behind her, "and we have to get to them."

"We?" I asked not without trepidation.

"The others have gone on ahead of me," she explained. "There were six of us from the Infirmary who volunteered to go. The others went on after I saw movement inside Lucas Terrace. I thought there might be someone still alive in there and was coming inside when you appeared."

"Did you see a woman at the door?" I asked without much hope. Abbie nodded.

"Yes. A Mrs. Quayle. She was taken back into town by one of our group. She asked if we'd seen her husband. Did you —" I interrupted her question with a shake of my head. She looked down, with her right hand wiped her cheek and down across her chin, softly, as if taking the news in carefully. "I understand," she whispered. "I'm sorry." I think that was for Mary Quayle.

"All right," I changed subjects. "If we have rescues to complete before our date, we'd better get on with it." Abbie looked at me curiously, then remembered, smiled.

"Yes. Our date." She smiled, shyly and of course perfectly, and for the second time on that godforsaken day she kissed me. It was her lips on mine this time, with a firmness of purpose that left me wanting to line up behind myself for more. It made the hurricane go away.

Then it came back.

We headed for the beach, generally south and the wind now at our back, which made heading into the peril much easier. A consoling thought. The storm had obliterated any landmark that would tell us we had gone a block or crossed a street or passed into a neighborhood, or anything that would tell us anything except that we were deep, deep in hell. To our right about a hundred yards we could see light in the darkness. It seemed to be a lantern or torch the way it flickered. If there was someone holding it, he or she or they were not benefiting much from it, to be sure. It was moving, as if it was afloat. Maybe someone had managed a raft out of the debris and would make it to high ground. Since there was no way for us to make a course to the light, we pushed forward. When I looked back a moment later, the light was gone from sight. Maybe just gone.

We walked for fifteen minutes, usually knee deep in the muck, occasionally noting a deeper hole by falling into it. Twice Abbie nearly disappeared from view, plummeting suddenly into a hidden crevice. My hand on her arm was all that kept us together. I found one hole all by myself, without help, and plunged up to my neck in the muddy liquid that now covered the entire earth. Abbie pulled with both hands on my arm until I could find a foothold below and wrench myself to safety. My shoulder expressed its general displeasure.

The darkness, somehow, got darker. It was sundown somewhere above the storm and night was falling over night. All we could see now were shadow things, mostly as they bobbed and floated by. The larger pieces – lumber now reclaimed as driftwood – I thwarted as they appeared; the smaller pieces – wire and glass and body parts – we allowed to bump and push away, too exhausted to attend to every item that confronted us.

We had both become incredibly tired. We plodded through the crud, deafened now to the howling, almost without any senses functioning except the one to hold on to each other and survive. We had seen no one – alive – since we left the Terrace. Perhaps we were the only ones left. Adam and Eve. Starting over. I was too tired to enjoy the image. Some

Garden, anyway. It was Genesis One-one now, not Two. My Momma had taught me well.

"In the beginning darkness covered the earth and the earth was without form, and void. And the spirit moved over the earth." Momma paused and looked down at my cherubic face, my eyes twisted up in a frown of the mystery. *"That was God looking down on everything,"* she gently explained. *"God would put everything in its place."* She would read in that soothing voice that mothers share with their children. We sat together on the tiny cot, the flaps of the tent folding and unfolding in the breeze that came off the Potomac. A lantern sat on the little table that was the only other furniture there. It was our dining table, bedside table, and whatever else it needed to be.

"And God created a Garden for the man to live in. And Adam lived and worked in the Garden, and walked side by side with God through the Garden every evening." Momma was still reading. I was half-asleep, with images of storms and birds and cattle and — my favorite part — creeping things creeping on the earth.

The snake curled itself around my left calf before I even knew that it was anywhere around. It had been submerged in the storm surge, probably doing what the rest of us living things were doing that night - trying to stay alive. Most had likely been unsuccessful so far. This one - black and about five feet long - had found something relatively firm to hang on to. My leg.

I raised my leg instinctively into the air as I felt the grip tighten. Abbie gasped and drew her hand away from mine. Stepped to her right. I reached for the serpent's head with my good right hand, squeezed my fingers hard just behind its throat and pulled at the same time. The snake resisted for a few seconds, then reluctantly relaxed its coils and went limp. I held it in the air, its frightened eyes darting back and forth in its head, as I stared at it from a few inches away. I didn't think it was poisonous. Probably a king snake. The ones I'd slept with in Cuba and Guatemala sleek and green and deadly - would've had me by now.

I dropped this one back into the sand slick that tugged up to my thighs, and it disappeared in an instant. I hoped it would make it through, although I decided not to share this with the angel beside me.

Except she was no longer beside me.

"Abbie!" I screamed at the top of my lungs, the power coming from some reservoir deep inside of me. I slammed my hand down on the surface of the splaying water to my right - where she had been standing only moments before, as if to send some urgent message echoing beneath the surface. "Where are you?!" I shouted as I reached down into the murky goo with both arms outstretched. Nothing. I took a step and reached down again. A third time. Sand sieved through my empty fingers.

Whatever miracles are manifested in moments of crisis, and whatever Source creates them, I may have lifted up some silent plea in that moment, I don't recall. I may have yelled it in some primal voice for that matter. That sound may have penetrated the hurricane and soared into the heavens above and beyond its fury. I don't know what or how.

But on the fourth try my hands grabbed wads of clothes and I pulled the angel to the surface. Abbie sputtered and shook and flailed at me as if I had been holding her under. She fought out of fear and anger and instinct. I pulled her to me, and just held on. Tighter, until she gave in, collapsing like a rag doll against my chest. She sobbed. I did, too. And we just stood there, the storm encompassing the whole world with its noise and passion. But we were temporarily oblivious to anything but each other and the precious hold we had on life.

"I have you now," I whispered in her ear. "We'll be all right." And I believed that.

We stood there until the wind pushed at us with a terrible gust. I lost my balance, threw one leg forward in the muck, straightened us up, held on. The water suddenly receded about a foot, down below my knees. I seized the opportunity to get my position as firm as I could. What was left of a foundation - the rest of the house no more than a stack of giant toothpicks some-where up the island, I supposed, peeked from the water, and in three strides we were atop the concrete floor. It felt good to have the water off our weary legs, even if for that moment.

I looked at Abbie with an eye for damage. She still sobbed and sniffed, but after a moment she brushed her soaked hair away from her face, gave her head a shake, blinked and smiled at me. Like the sun coming out. What was left of her dress hung wilted against her body, wrapped at her legs like bandages, one shoulder bared to the elements. But she stood erect, her hand tightly wound into mine. She was healing me in that instant.

In the darkness of the storm-wrapped night, we both peered toward the beach, our destination. We had walked less than five hundred yards from the shambles that had been Lucas Terrace. We had a thousand yards to go. But we would never get there.

6

It loomed there in front of us, like a Satan's Tower of metal and wood and human flesh. It scratched the clouds above with its razor edge parapet. It projected a darkness far deeper and blacker than the nighttime that had fallen on the hurricane. Even the storm itself, which had created this monstrosity, seemed unwilling to claim it: the waters fell prostrate to this horrible god, so great and terrible at the same time. The winds made their way around it, unable to penetrate its mass, uncertain of its power.

Abbie and I stood frozen in speechless awe, staring upward, our necks craning until they hurt. But we couldn't take our eyes off the thing; it pulled at us even as it repulsed. Layer after layer of shattered homes, beachside buildings, trolleys, and what had once been people, all stacked in a grotesque pattern that only the most evil Architect could devise. Across its face a twisted smile, the remnants of the tram tracks that had once - just hours before - wound down from Mechanic Street to the Midway. They had been lifted out of their moorings by the storm surge, become a scythe that cut its way across the end of the island, slicing every home at its roots. Driftwood and bodies gathered up, pushed along without mercy, stacking, building itself up, acting as some amoral Judge and everyone and everything was condemned to die.

It had made those screeching noises I had heard a mile away before. Behind it I guessed there was nothing but a barren landscape, the sea and sand joining forces across miles of the island city. As far as I could see to my left and right through the pitch of night the monster stood and glared at the remainder of Galveston. It seemed as if it would lick its putrid lips in anticipation of consuming more before the dawn came.

In that mesmerizing, terrifying moment, it had ground to a halt.

The two of us stood at its base for what seemed an eternity, unable to dislodge ourselves from this spectacle. We held each other as tightly as we dared, knowing that at the next instant the Thing would come suddenly alive, growling and hungering, and sweep us into its yawning orifice as it had a thousand before us.

Finally Abbie's hand slid up to my elbow and squeezed. It was as if someone had startled me back to life. I turned and saw the fear in her eyes, a reflection of my own face?

I managed an unconvincing smile. "Are you ready to go? I think dinner is waiting."

"Take me away from it," she whispered. "Please."

I reached across and took her by the shoulder, turned her gently away from the brigand mass, and we stepped from the concrete piling back into what had once been a city street. I kept my arm around her waist, and she folded hers against her breast. We walked in the ankle-deep seawater, and never looked back. Would we have turned to salt?

We walked with conviction for an hour, north and toward what may have still been left of civilization on this bedraggled isle. Into the wind, the course was brutal. The tiniest of objects flew at us like wasps, buzzing and bruising and stinging. Never a warning. We saw no one, heard no voices, no screams. Just as strangely, we came across no bodies. If we walked past the ruins of Lucas Terrace, neither of us noticed or if she did she said nothing.

We may as well have been walking on the surface of the moon, the only humans on that orb, abandoned by our world, left to trudge eternally in no direction to nowhere. The hour seemed to be a night in length.

It must have been after ten when we saw the first light, a flicker of other life out here. The lantern cast its tiny shadow at the sill of the infirmary window, then vanished in the outer darkness that drifted everywhere else we could see. It was yet fifty yards away, but we would make that leg.

I pulled Abbie closer, if that was physically possible, and pointed with my good arm. I put my lips to her ear and said, "Home." Her right hand careened up to my face and stroked my cheek, once, then returned to its sanctuary at her bosom. Heaven's touch.

Mr. Scott was gone. One of the nurses said he had headed into the city to get more help. Others had been filling in during his absence. There were sixty or more cots scattered in great order over the big room, a semblance of being lined up, I supposed on second thought. Each had a person lying in repose, a blanket for nearly everyone. A dozen aides wandered among the beds or sat beside one. No one spoke, no sound except the shuffling of feet, the tearing of cloth bandages, an occasional groan or snore. The wind howled outside and provided whatever musical background was currently available. It was a sound so incessant, so insistent, as to render a melancholy over the whole hospital. A young man looked forlornly toward one of the boarded windows as if to say, Please stop that noise before we are all driven mad. The storm paid no heed.

Two nurses came up to us as we stepped inside, offering to help us to a cot or chair, but silently, motioning, extending hands to us. I accepted one offer and turned to Abbie. She was looking across the room, spotted someone she thought might be there, ignored the offer of help, and brushed past as she almost hurried to her destination. I watched, amazed, as she managed the obstacle course of cots until she came to one on the far end of the room. She stopped. Looked down. Smiled. Knelt on the floor beside a small figure curled down at the end of the makeshift bed. A patch of blond hair peeked from the blanket, nothing else to identify its contents. Abbie began to stroke the little child's hair, so gently as to not wake her from her sleep.

I had never seen anything as beautiful.

I was led to an empty cot against the inside wall, and I accepted the lead without resistance. A blanket had been launched over my drenched - and throbbing - shoulders as I walked. I gathered it around in front of me with my one good hand, the broken wrist limp at my side. I sat at the edge of the cot only long enough to look across the room at the angel once more, then fell over onto the bed, asleep before I got there.

7

The herd came first as a rumble, on the other side of the rise. We could hear but not see, but we all knew. A stampede! It was the high country of Montana Territory, and the sun-drenched prairie rose and fell for a million miles in every direction. Waves of summer grasses tantalized the cattle and fattened them for the fall roundup.

Twenty of us lounged around the campsite, some standing by the chuck wagon, others around the fire with a tin of coffee in hand. It was just first light, and Montana summer mornings were still brisk enough for ponchos and steaming coffee. One of the cow punchers practiced whipping his lariat, aiming it indiscreetly at a tent post. If he hit his target the tent would come down and someone would have to take the time and effort to get up from the fire and go kick his ass. We hoped he kept missing.

I had been in the high meadows for six weeks, learning the trade. Not much more than a snot nose beginner, at seventeen I was older than *half the company. At my age most cowboys had been on the trail for three years, maybe four. I had broken a bone in my leg the first day with the herd, too eager to impress by leaping off my mount before the sorrel came to a stop, jamming my boot down on an unforgiving rock and snapping something inside just below my knee. I still gimped around some, but an ornery splint and a bad attitude - mostly from embarrassment - had healed it up pretty fast.*

Now I stood halfway between wagon and fire, an empty cup in hand, as the sound bore down upon the camp. I looked up with everyone else, but we had no doubt what was coming. This was no rolling thunder. This was a maddened herd of 4,500 cattle on their way through us. Whatever had spooked them we might never know. Right now we didn't care.

Tin cups and blankets flew. Shouts emanated from half a dozen, some giving instructions, I suppose. We all broke and ran, guessing which direction and how much ground would get us out of the stampede's route. I could run but it wasn't my best skill after the leg had broken, and I was dragging behind the others when the first heads appeared over the rise. Reds and browns, a smattering of longhorns thrown in, they came on hard, fast, crazed, without control, fifty wide and hundreds deep waiting just over the horizon to trample what was left in the wake.

The herd blasted into the camp. The chuck wagon tilted in slow motion then catapulted over, rolling over onto its back. The campfire exploded under a hundred hooves, blankets and bedrolls tossed like confetti into the air. I looked over my shoulder as I ran perpendicular to the front line of the stampede. I wasn't going to make it outside the fiery edge. A longhorn led his battalion at me, charging, snorting, eyes blazened, twenty more right on his heels.

He came right at me, the thunder deafening, the dust kicked up ahead of the herd. Into the camp they came on. I looked up just as the boy fell beneath the tumbling hooves, in the infirmary door, stumbling across the cots, nurses screaming -

"Will!" I woke up in a cold sweat, sat straight up in my cot, both arms extended in front of me to stop the apparitions that charged from my nightmare. My shoulders heaved, the blanket slid off onto the floor. A nurse ran to my side, put her hand on my arm to comfort. Then Abbie stood before me, leaning, bent at the knees, her face in mine. She touched my face with her magic fingers, made it all go away.

"Who is Will?" she asked in a soothing tone.

"What?"

"You cried out for Will. Who is Will?" she asked again. I shook my head, tried to remember the dream. Snatches of it. Cattle, blankets flying, a boy running behind me, where did the boy come from? Will. Not the boy in the snow storm, though.

"Will Murney," I exclaimed.

"Uh huh," the angel encouraged me with her eyes to go on.

"Will Murney," I said again, as if to remind myself and make the name stick. "I saw him at the convent today. His friends,"

I began to babble, "the nuns. Ropes, the children. My God." I was breathing hard again. Abbie sat on the cot beside me and wrapped an arm around the back of my shoulders. The separated one pounded a steady rhythm of pain. Abbie's left hand was in my lap. I took it in mine. Looked at her.

"I put him on some driftwood, Abbie," I explained in a weak voice. "They floated away. I left them out there in the storm. I have to find them." I started up from the cot. My knees buckled and I decided sitting back down was a better idea.

"He'll be all right, Cale," she said. "God will watch over him. You tried to help him. You did what was necessary." Consoling. With meaning. Like she believed it.

"I have to know, Abbie. I have to find him."

"Tomorrow, Cale," she decided. "Tomorrow we'll go look for Will Murney. Listen," she said with some excitement in her voice, "listen to the storm."

I listened. The howling was gone. It was eerily quiet outside the walls of the infirmary. I hadn't heard that much silence in -

"What time is it? How long have I been out?" I asked no one in particular.

"After midnight," came a man's voice from the middle of the room. Two hours?

"The sun will shine tomorrow, Cale," Abbie's honey voice was so wonderful. "We'll look tomorrow. Now you need to rest.

I'll stay here beside you." An offer for the ages. Being an idiot, I didn't accept it.

"No," I said almost too simply, matter-of-factly. "I have to find him, Abbie. Now." She looked at me without expression. The nurse turned and walked away, probably disgusted with me. Didn't blame her.

"I'll be back," I said close to her face, almost whispering. "I'll find Will and I'll find you again." Abbie sat back, away from me, stared down at her hands folded in her lap. As if counting to ten. I waited. Also for my knees to get ready this time when I stood. They were ready, I decided, but her hand reached for mine before I moved.

"All right," she said. "I'll go with you."

"No," I protested, sure of myself this time. "You must stay here. I cannot risk you again, not out there. I'll come back for you."

She let me finish my say. Smiled. "I'll not lose you, Cale Lincoln."

We said goodbye to several of the nurses who walked us to the door. Abbie had spent another minute at the far end of the infirmary with a little child. I don't think she ever knew her name. Nor would ever forget her.

When we walked outside, the world had changed. For the better. Clouds still fumed above, but they seemed thinner somehow, even though we could hardly make them out. Well past midnight now. The wind had died, down but not out. Closer to what was normal on this island. Water still pooled everywhere; the rain was intermittent though the showers were hard.

Clusters of people stood in doorways along Broadway as we neared the edge of the Strand district. A few phantom souls moved through the streets, like us. Most of the buildings in this area still stood, windows busted out, roofs half gone, outdoor tables and booths in shambles, piles of bricks by the millions, I guessed.

Every half block or so, we would see an entire building - or what was left of it - shattered and piled on itself. The storm had been discriminating, picking its victims here out of the crowded structures, tumbling them into nothing more than refuse. We picked out the water levels on the sides of the homes, some waist high. Fences leaned; street posts bowed. Trees bent, many broke, some uprooted and showing their vulnerable underbellies for all to see.

These made me think of Will Murney and his two friends. Kept me going.

Abbie kept up the pace with me, stride for stride. She had long since hiked up her skirt to the middle of her knees, shed her boots for sandals that someone had found for her. Her hair she pulled up on top of her head, wrapped, not neatly, with a ribbon torn from the back of her dress. She had scrapes and bruises on her face and neck, mud caked on her calves and the back of her arms. A deep scratch across her throat still seemed angry, red. A hair pin connected her dress at the shoulder. She was the most beautiful vision on earth. I, on the other hand, looked like hell.

But the pains and the throbbing were gone. Or I'd put them aside. I didn't hurt anywhere except inside. A thick cloth wrapped my wrist. My shoulder I ignored. I had more tears on my skin than my clothes, but I'd quit bleeding long before. I was on a mission, and nothing would stop me. Except not finding him. Needle in a haystack. Middle of the night. A hundred square miles of sand and sea. And no clue where to start.

So I'd started where I was. I would cut across the highest level of the island, where things were in some semblance of order, where the city's outline still made sense. Then, if we hadn't found him, we'd crisscross wherever we were able, ask the people we saw, call out his name in the alleys and the empty buildings that still stood.

Abbie and I hardly spoke. We directed all of our energy to walking, covering distances, a sense of accomplishment at each street intersection, the end of each city block. We held hands most of the time, but every once in awhile one of us would turn off our path and look into a pile of rubble, or speak to someone who cowered on a porch.

We walked for two hours. Impossibly. We had no reserve for this. But we did it anyway. We couldn't not do it. One boy, we might have asked ourselves? A complete stranger? So many others? Didn't matter. I promised Will he would be all right. I would see him again. Promises made.

As we made our way south from Broadway, sometime after two o'clock on Sunday morning, a remarkable event occurred: the stars came out. Well, not exactly the Milky Way that my mother had told stories about, but at least something up there was twinkling, a cloud break. The awful storm was passing to our north, taking out its frustration on Houston or somewhere else in Texas. Maybe it was heading for New Orleans soon. No way of knowing. Didn't care. It was leaving the island.

Or was it? Maybe this was the eye of the damn thing, some monstrous Cyclops sense of humor: calm and clear and hopeful, then the next barrage still waiting off the coast. The sense of urgency hit me again like a blow to the solar plexus. Find the boys.

Abbie and I turned onto a street whose name had been blown to kingdom come along with most of its inhabitants. We were two blocks away from Broadway, had seen a blown-down sign that said 30th Street on what was left of it not far from here, and guessed our general location. Wise beyond my years.

We walked one block back to the east when we glimpsed what looked like a building still more or less intact. Lanterns

— three, four — were swinging from some rampart about ten feet off the ground, making eerie shadows dance in a breeze that kept kicking up. People were moving beneath the lanterns, in and out of the light. I couldn't make out how many or who they might be until we had come within about fifty feet of the structure. Then I understood.

It was a store. On the side it said in broad, dark letters: **DRUG STORE**. They were looting it.

Never bothering to look over their shoulders, the men — I rough-counted three of them now — would climb in through the shattered front glass window, now a gaping hole, and come back out a minute later loaded with boxes. These they would stack out on what was more or less the sidewalk: they had kicked away a clear spot where mud and sand had been. The stack was already four boxes high by that many wide and long — a pretty good haul so far. It occurred to me briefly that they might be merchants trying to save the goods inside. But my instinct thought that was a bit naïve of me. The store was in good enough shape to be a better warehouse than out in the street. I could have made other arguments one way or the other, but that would have been a waste of energy. I knew who they were and what was going on.

We had stopped in the shadows to watch the pageant. Abbie started to speak but I shushed her. Lovingly. She instantly understood, her eyes wide with concern. Not fear, I noticed. What a girl. I nodded in the direction of a pile of rubble to our left, mostly bricks and chunks of concrete, and walked her to a spot that placed the debris between her and the thugs I was going to chat with in a moment. She didn't resist, but she was frowning very deeply at me as I let go of her hand and walked toward the lantern light.

As I walked I drew my good right hand around to my side and felt the pistol that, miraculously, still resided on its belt. I hadn't thought of the gun for hours, hadn't needed to, I suppose. Now I would. Why I hadn't lost it in the storm was beyond me. Those kinds of questions often were.

I carried a Colt .38 automatic A&N, "New Army" they called it, a Model 1892 modified four years later. Teddy Roosevelt gave it to me after Kettle Hill. He had used it on our run up that rise, killed one Spaniard and wounded another that I took care of a moment later when he had the colonel in his sights. TR thanked me for saving his life, gave me the pistol.

As I made my way into the light, one of the looters turned and saw me. He put down the box cradled in his arms, stepped over it in my direction, and stood, legs braced straight, knees locked, ready for action. Or to be fitted for a new suit. He looked right between my eyes. I stopped. Returned his friendly glance. We were fifteen feet apart.

"Whaddaya want, mister?" he asked elegantly. Well brought up. "Ya got no business here," he continued his welcoming speech. "Better just move on."

I thought I would try to jump into this delightful conversation if he would just give me a break. "Just out taking a midnight stroll," I explained, trying to keep that same happy air about our conversation. "The owners of the store here know you've come to help them?" I inquired. I had no clue who the owners might be, but he didn't know that.

"None of your damn business, far as I can tell," he replied. He said can like it was kin. Quaint. "Git going, if you know what's good fer ya." The English language took another beating.

"Guess I can't do that," I said slowly, my hand resting gingerly on my hip, fingers folded into a fist.

"You know what kind of trouble you're getting into?" I was fairly sure, but decided not to let on. I shook my head no, but I made sure my smile was pleasant.

"Perhaps you could tell me," I invited.

"You dumb sonavabitch," he said, his teeth clenched. With that, what appeared to be the end of our tete-a-tete, he reached behind his back to retrieve what I could only assume was a gun. I was a world quicker.

I shot him in the right shoulder, right where I aimed. The sound echoed off the store front and the cubic yards of debris, sounded like a repeating Winchester. He dropped in his tracks, legs no longer straight, with only a grunt when he hit the street. I took one step toward him, my gun still pointed at the sorry lump of humanity.

The other looters flushed from the store like a covey of quail, scrambling out through the window opening, somersaulting to the ground as they lost their balance, regaining their feet, more or less, and kind of crabwalking into the darkness. One looked back at me, the other didn't.

I stood over the one I'd shot. He'd live. I had mixed emotions.

Abbie and I walked on.

8

I found Will Murney at 3:30 in the morning. He was walking
down a dark street, shirtless and shoeless, his ripped breeches
folded up to his knees. His hair was tousled, but dry. He had
gained a limp during the night, and it looked like the bottom of
his foot might be badly cut. He was staring down at the street
directly in front of each step he was taking. Never looked up. Just
trying to move forward.

Abbie and I had spent another hour or so on our trek. We
had seen very few people, live ones, but piles of the dead. After
awhile every block, every corner was just the same – brick piles,
sand, mud, driftwood, and bodies. We had stopped at the first of
the dead we came across. Abbie insisted. Checked to see if any
still breathed. No signs of life. Some were already bloating and
chalk white, stiff. Others like rag dolls. When we would find

someone out in the middle of a street I would carry the body over to the side, put it on a window sill or a flat board or with other bodies. Old, young, men and women, some so battered by the hurricane we could only tell they were human. Had been.

One woman had been driven through a wrought iron fence, wedged there by the furious sea, her long blonde hair tangled impossibly around one fence post. I left her there.

We saw arms and legs dangling from beneath huge piles of house parts. I tried to move them, but finally would give up. It would take ten men. And equipment. And daylight.

The worst was finding the children. We both let the tears stream down our faces as we walked through the town that had become a makeshift cemetery. We didn't sob or cry or make any sounds. The tears just came.

And then they stopped. We both had run out for that night. Maybe forever. We hadn't even spoken a word for that hour.

I was getting up off my knees beside the body of an old Negro man when I saw a ghost meandering toward me, face down, bent over, arms dangling without purpose, kind of zigzagging without much objective. Abbie squeezed my arm. I nodded. Tapped the butt of my pistol with two fingers. Just to be sure. We waited. The apparition came out of the darkness, right at us, right up to us. I was prepared to step aside when I realized it was just a boy, so I let him bump into me. He didn't even react, just collapsed into me. I wrapped my arms around him as he dropped, in one movement brought him up off the ground, his head dangling like it was going to fall off. I gathered him up closer against me, his head nestled in the crook of my elbow. He was already unconscious. I looked at his face.

It was Will.

I looked over at Abbie. Smiled a crooked, weary smile. She wrinkled her forehead, looked at the boy, back at me. Understood. Stepped over to my side, brushed a lock of hair from his face. "Hello, Will Murney," she said.

I had done what I set out to do. I could take almost no credit for being smart enough or skillful enough to have accomplished finding Abbie again or Will Murney again. They had both found me. A peculiar world, this one. But a world I was more than happy to be in at that moment, despite the terror-stricken tragedy that surrounded us. Exactly where we were was another consideration, and where we would go next added on to that list. A northerly course, cut through a side street if possible, should bring us back to high ground. The infirmary was two miles away, but there were other alternatives. Safe, quiet, peopled, dry, food and water, those seemed to be the first criteria.

We started our return to civilization. The most direct route, given my general ignorance of the city, that is, seemed to just be following the star that we could see above. The wind had shifted, was at our back. Clouds continued to roil but without the same anger. They were related to their furious cousins who had come through earlier, but the breeze seemed to be the old home one, the one that belonged here. It even had a special aroma to it, a salty sea breeze straight from the Caribbean. But there was another set of smells that began to lift up also. I didn't care to identify these. Didn't have to.

If we retraced any of our steps that next hour we didn't recognize it. We were cutting across our longer search route, I think on 26th Street but with little way of confirmation. When we reached what I believed was Broadway, a huge two-story home collapsed right beside us. No warning. No creaking sounds. It just fell, its wide front porch sluicing out in front from under the toppling structure. Glass exploded somewhere inside, a chandelier perhaps. Mud and grass flew. I threw my arm up over Will's still unconscious form, and mud splattered my left side. Abbie was on my right at that moment, and spared the added mess.

A piece of metal, bronze I think, popped from the house as it crashed, bounced crazily once and spun like a child's top right at our feet. I looked down at it. There were letters embossed on it. Abbie reached and picked it up, pulled it close to where we could see. "McLeod," it said. I looked over at what had been someone's home. No more. Abbie dropped the bronze sign. It clanged for an instant when it hit.

We turned right, walked several more blocks, and headed for the silhouettes of several buildings, all in a row, all in what appeared to be good shape. They were homes, large, impressive structures, mortar and brick and turrets and fences. A few windows were blown out, several trees broken and dying in the yards, and a water line about knee high. Otherwise, little damage.

Across Broadway from these homes was what had been a church, now demolished by the giant. The tip of its steeple lay at an awkward angle atop the rubble. Part of one wall still stood, precariously, a rounded gape where a stained glass window had been preparing to light Mass at dawn. The storm had been fickle and evil here, sparing homes and crushing a sanctuary. One of the homes would now have to suffice.

The first two houses on the left were dark and I supposed empty. We needed shelter, but we needed some help, too. We needed a place with people who could make bandages, clean us up, feed us. Clean water all of a sudden seemed like nectar of the gods, and we were not on Olympus. Not yet.

The third house, on our left, was lit up like a candelabra. It rose high into the sky, more than three floors, with chimneys and turrets poking at the stars. Every window seemed intact, and inside every window light was beaming. Flickering shadows told me there were people in most of those rooms, as well, moving back and forth between the lamps and the outside. Where we were. But not for long.

In the front of the mansion a fence struck a foreboding line of defense against the rest of the world. In the center its one accommodation to that world, a double-wide gate through which a tram car could have easily glided. One side of the gate was pulled open, allowing plenty of room for the three of us to walk inside, up the cobbled walk, and to the base of an impressive, though taxing at that moment, concrete stairway. Abbie and I never hesitated. One step, eight, twelve. Will still asleep in my arms. To the smallish porch and the front door of the haven we sought.

The door was ajar, and I started to kick at it when Abbie stepped in front of me and knocked against the ornate glass at its center. Ever courteous, she. Almost immediately the door pulled open. A curious image stood there. A tall, handsome Negro in full formal butler attire, tails and black tie against a starched white shirt, high-collared, pinstripe pants hanging straight down to the polished black boots. He bowed slightly at the waist as a greeting, and in the same motion turned his hip away and motioned with an exceptionally long arm for us to come inside. As he turned we saw what was likely a housemaid standing just behind his shoulder, half his size, black and white dress with apron starched and unwrinkled. She had a pleasant smile, although it may have been pasted on there some years earlier. It had a slightly worn look at its edges.

A paradox, but somehow I wasn't surprised. Abbie stepped inside ahead of me, and I followed with the boy in my arms. Both of our greeters looked quietly at the sleeping boy I carried, little reaction. As I passed the tall houseman, he said crisply but warmly in my direction, "Welcome to the colonel's home." Thank you, I thought but didn't say.

We stepped into a round foyer that spilled visitors into a long, ornately designed hallway. The wood on its walls was mahogany, I guessed, with intricately-patterned glass pressed into its sides at intervals. As we took several steps inside, I saw two openings right and left. Both led to parlors. The one on the right dark-paneled like its hallway cousin, the left somewhat lighter in tone. In a glance I noticed that both had fireplaces. Cozy warm in the winter. At the end of the hall I could barely make out the base of a curling, spiraling staircase. Also dark wood.

I registered the thought that the floor was slippery, and wondered if the water had made its way into this palatial manse. Maybe I would ask. Later.

I could hear voices, people in back rooms off to both sides. Will Murney stirred in my arms. I looked down at his peaceful, sleeping face. He blinked several times, quickly, as if something inside was rousing him. He opened his eyes, closed them as if it had been too difficult an enterprise, then opened them again. Looked up at me.

"Good morning," I said. He smiled a crooked smile, barely registering the words, the fact that he was alive a coming revelation.

"Hey," he replied in a soft, cracked voice. "Aren't you that guy -?" I nodded. "Cale," I said simply. "Hey," he repeated. He squirmed a bit, his body contemplating whether it should right itself or just lay where it was mighty comfortable at the moment.

"Let's get you somewhere you can rest," I invited. He lay his head back in the crook of my arm.

I looked up to reconnoiter the palace we had found. A tall, gray-headed gentleman — sometimes that word just seemed to apply – had appeared seemingly out of nowhere. He stood erect, pushing against sixty years with defiance, gallantly clad in a three-piece pinstripe blue suit, immaculate starched white shirt, buttoned to the throat, no tie. Ordinarily I would be taller than him by several inches, although at the moment he towered over me. He looked at me, then Will, then past me at Abbie the vision. Smiled three different, personally-tuned smiles. He bowed ever so slightly, enough to make the point.

"Colonel Walter Gresham, at your service," he said in a hard, smooth voice. "Welcome to my castle." Interesting.

9

The name was familiar, but I couldn't put my finger on why. I couldn't deal with my own name very well at 4:30 in the morning. I made an attempt.

"Caleb Lincoln," I managed. He nodded. "Will Murney," I glanced at the sleeping boy in my arms.

"Abigail Scarborough," a lilting voice of gentility said behind me. Angels' wings.

"I am most pleased to make your acquaintance." He would have tipped a hat if he had had one on. "My wife Josephine and I extend the hospitality of our home to you. Please tell us what we can do for you." He paused. "Are any of you injured in any way?"

My broken wrist scowled. My previously separated shoulder hummed its Jamaican tune. Every bone and muscle volunteered. My knees buckled. The butler came up from behind in an instant, reached two powerful arms under my arms. Colonel Gresham stepped forward at the same time and offered his hands to take the boy. Will, still asleep, rolled out of my grasp and into the colonel's, who lifted him up and away as if he were no more than a bouquet of flowers.

I would have carried Will Murney for the rest of my life if it had come to that, but he was in good hands still. I didn't begrudge the help. The colonel motioned with the merest shake of his head and the butler had stood me back up and was at the colonel's side.

"Joshua, take this young man to my room upstairs and put him in my bed. On your way, please show these folks where they can rest." He lowered his voice. "Take them where the rest of the crowd won't bother them." Joshua nodded, yessir. Took Will, light as a feather. Started down the hall. Looked over his shoulder as an invitation. Abbie stepped forward and slid her hand under my arm.

"Thank you, colonel," she said in honey. "You are so kind to take us in."

"I only wish I could do more, ma'am," he replied graciously. "We were blessed to be saved from the wrath, and must do our part."

"How many are here?" she inquired.

"I've lost the exact count," he said. He frowned. "Perhaps seventy-five or so, if I were to hazard a guess." I raised my eyebrows.

"We've plenty of room, however. Most are in the drawing room which you will see to your left as you reach the stairs. Others have made their way to the second and third floors. The children's rooms will stand the crowd."

"Your children are all right?" Abbie ventured, concern in her voice.

"Our children, thank you very much for asking, are all grown and gone now. Only Mrs. Gresham and I were here when the storm came in. Fortunately, a visit from several of our grandchildren had only recently concluded, and they are safe on the mainland." Abbie smiled. The colonel returned it. I stood like a busted lamp post.

"Now, young lady," Gresham said in a fatherly stern voice, "you and Mr. Lincoln follow Joshua. Get some rest. The day will dawn soon and the salvation of our fair city will be the task at hand." And with that, he turned on a heel and disappeared into the room to our left.

Joshua was already halfway down the hall, Will's legs and arms extended where we could see them, dangling like stalks of wheat. Abbie prodded me into following after. I tried to be gallant but my legs did not feel the need to cooperate, so most of the hallway was traversed in some fool's parade: me stumbling forward, the angel keeping our collective balance.

Joshua paused at the base of the stairs. We caught up to him and both of us stared upward. The stairway spiraled high into the throat of Gresham's castle, alongside an enormous internal tower. We could make out balconies along the way up, and an occasional voice or two that came wafting down from somewhere up there. I supposed there were dozens of people at every level.

To our left, a bright parlor opened up. It was filled with people milling about. Their attires suggested the various ways in which they had battled the storm, from ragged and torn to clean and starched. Most in-between. They made a common noise that suggested a somber party. Several faces turned toward us as we came in view. Blank looks. Unrecognizing. Uncaring. I remember seeing no children.

I turned and stared back up the yawning chasm that awaited us. The steps may have numbered in the thousands, or so it seemed at that moment, a daunting prospect. But just as I inhaled and readied my legs for the journey, Joshua turned aside to our right, still holding the limp urchin, and walked around the stairwell and into the shadows. I noticed the fireplace — yet another — at the base of the stairs as we walked by, and a huge mahogany turret at the first turn of the spiral way.

Abbie and I rounded the dark corner to find where Joshua had gone. The ceiling suddenly lowered as if we would crawl under the stairs. Then a door, opened, followed through, a small mud room the size of a walk-in closet. Two doors from which to choose. A tiny lantern above dimly lighting our position. Joshua chose the door to his right, pushed on it with a knee. It swung open casually. We kept up. A slightly larger room awaited on the other side.

Simple. Whitewashed walls. No pictures. Nothing ornate. No stained glass. No murals. Square, high windows, hardwood floor.

The servants' quarters. At the far end of the smallish room were its only pieces of furniture. A wash basin, a small dresser with four drawers wider than they were deep or high, and a double bed. No four-poster. No headboard.

Joshua turned as he stepped to the center of the room. Nodded at us. "I'll put the boy in the room next door," he turned his head an inch toward another door that I now saw on the right hand wall. "He'll be fine there. I'll wash his face. There are blankets." And Joshua vanished.

I had thought about objecting: this was most likely Joshua's own room and he would have to fend for himself. But my next thought was that he would not be sleeping this night anyway. Two thoughts seemed to be my current limit.

Abbie pushed my elbow and the rest of me followed to the bed. I half-fell to the mattress, shoving a blanket more or less out of the way. Twisted onto my back, my feet dangling off the side. Abbie knelt gently on the floor beside me, caressed my forehead, whispered soothing sounds near my ear.

I reached my arm around her waist and pulled her up and onto the mattress beside me, shifting my weight until she nestled against my side, her arms curled on my chest, her head on my shoulder. I had one arm underneath her, the other wrapped over her. It pulled her closer to me. Her face and mine an inch apart.

Our lips met in that fraction that had been between us, soft at first, then harder, with determination, a spark of desire from deep within where neither believed it could have survived what we'd been through. A shiver ran through her body and I could feel the tremor as if it were mine. I pulled a little closer, kissed her harder. She responded with reserves from somewhere, wherever women keep them.

We paused just long enough to take a breath, our mouths a millimeter apart.

"Some date," I whispered.

"Better late than," she murmured. The millimeter disappeared.

10

The *thump* woke me, even through the roar of the wind outside. It sounded like a sack of flour tossed from the back of
a wagon, and being sound asleep it seemed to come at me from a
distance. But I wasn't that sound asleep that I didn't recognize it
for it what it had to be: it was a body.

I sat up in the bed. The first hint of dawn crept into the
high windows above me. I looked down to see Abbie still
asleep. We had covered a remarkable amount of ground in the
previous two hours, getting to know each other. It had been
an inch at a time, painstaking detail, with whispers and kisses
and touches. When I finally fell asleep I was fairly certain I
had not missed a place.

With less than a half hour of sleep, I now found myself amaz-
ingly alert. It was that sound. Too familiar.

I rose from the bed, slipped pants and boots on as quietly as I could, pulled a torn shirt over my head, and secured my pistol in the waistband, in front, hidden by the shirttails. Abbie slept on her right side, her face turned to the wall. She breathed evenly, deeply. Her hair scattered over the pillow and her shoulders, the blanket cozied up under her arms. I could see the outline of her legs, curled up beneath the folds.

I stepped to the door, pulled it open and went into the ante-room, retracing the steps we had taken two hours before. The sound of shuffling feet and loud whispers increased as I got closer to the commotion. Another door into the recesses of the hall behind the stairwell, then around.

A crowd was already gathering, some in bedclothes, others still dressed and wandering over from the parlor. The lamps still flickered brightly in the high-ceilinged foyer where I stood with the others, the hurricane whistled against the windows.

I followed the line where most of the crowd stared, up and toward the stairs. The body of a man hung limp on the mahogany turret where the stairs turned one last time before reaching ground level. He was bent completely in half, sagged, arms akimbo, head lolling in the last shivers of death. A woman gasped. I saw her hand go to her mouth in horror.

I looked past the body and up to the balconies above. Faces turned down, staring back at us. Five, six, then a seventh. One man seemed to grimace, or was he squinting for a better look? He had a shock of red hair that fell past his ears as he gaped.

I stepped into the crowd, and they parted quickly: no one seemed to want to get any closer to the body and were obliged to let me through. I took the steps two at a time. Impressing the ladies with derring-do, no doubt. Fearless. Five strides had me at level with the dead man, now still. Dead weight.

I looked up again, trying to guess where he had started his last, brief journey. A banister on the third floor looked bent, jutted out a foot into the air, calling attention to itself. I made a mental note, an accomplishment. He had apparently leaned against the weak railing, it had given way and he had hurtled to his death. In the aftermath of a terrible, killing storm, this person had survived all the elements had to throw at him, only to die ignominiously from a faulty beam. Gruesome irony, that.

I reached over and grabbed his shoulders, lifted against all the weight, which made the task ten times harder, but pulled him off the turret. The body gained its own momentum and slumped to the stairs where I stood, on its back. The legs hung awkwardly, and one arm pinned underneath the torso. I figured the fall had broken every rib, crushed organs, likely snapped the neck.

I bent down over the body. Blood stained the collar of the white shirt. I glanced up to see dark stains on the turret, on the stairs where the body had tumbled over. I looked back at the body. The face was of a man perhaps nearing thirty, pocked, eyes now wide in death. He was fully dressed, black pants and brown boots, suspenders which had snapped loose and now lay strewn against his waist. A slip of paper peeked from his front pants pocket. I absentmindedly reached for it, put it in my pocket without thinking.

"Is he dead?" a voice called out from the still crowd. The obvious hovering in the air like thick smoke, I still instinctively placed my hand against his neck to check for a pulse. My fingers poked about for several seconds. I drew my hand back when the realization sank in. Blood was smeared across my fingers and palm. I looked out over the crowd, who expected the official word.

"He's dead, all right," I said evenly. "He's been shot."

Part Two

Houston, September 15, 1900, 1:00 P.M.

11

"You're a Pinkerton man?" he asked incredulously. I nodded. "Wow!" he said.

Will Murney and I were sitting across a small crate from one another, both cross-legged although he seemed a lot more comfortable at it than me. Cards lay all over the top of the box: I had finally convinced myself that I was *letting* him win the poker game. Either that or it was some kind of Grand Punishment for playing cards in the basement of the German Methodist Church. He had me by two boxes of matches, ten million dollars and counting.

"Tell me about it," he exclaimed, his attention fixed on me. "Did you shoot anybody?"

"No," I said much to his obvious disappointment. No blood, no glory. "But I got my man," I added hopefully. That helped. Some.

Allan Pinkerton had hired me back as an operative in the spring of 1899 after my return from Cuba. I immediately left New York City and headed for Denver where I met with James McParland, superintendent of the detective agency in the western states. Mac and I got along well, and he sent me straightway to St. Louis to meet up with Charlie Siringo. Charlie was working out of Chicago and had a reputation across the West for finishing the job. He was working a train robbery case on the Texas-Arkansas border and needed someone to "go inside." That would be me. "Wow, train robbers," Will said.

I went to Hot Springs, posed as a peddler of snake oil, complete with creaky wagon and glossy banners to hang overhead. For two weeks I traveled around the countryside, generally making a nuisance of myself, although I made over $200 selling that coal tar-in-a-jar. I also listened. What I heard was that the Owens brothers, Carroll and Jake, had been throwing some money around lately, money they couldn't have earned off their pitiful truck farm. Most folks agreed the boys were no accounts.

I made sure I was at a saloon one evening when they romped in, already drunk, flinging dollar coins at the bartender and two of the upstairs ladies. I stole a quick look in Will's direction. He was listening. The part about the ladies didn't seem to disturb him. Wise beyond his years. *When they started pushing and shoving their way around, I held on to the bar top with a grip that left marks. Shooting them right then would have solved one problem, brought on a mess more.*

I wired Charlie Siringo when I had enough information, and told him to come down and we'd put the boys away. He came down and we put them away. "C'mon, Cale. Don't skip the good stuff." All right.

Siringo was a wiry little guy, not five foot nine and sure not 160 pounds. But built like a railroad spike. He'd chased down some of the best-known crooks in the west over the years, even wrote a book about it, something about Texas cowboys. Good man, on your side.

I met him at the train station outside Texarkana. He had a double holster with two revolvers, and a Winchester. Will's eyes brightened. The good stuff, coming right up. *We kept an eye on the brothers for two more days and night, until Charlie thought we could go ahead. Met them at a saloon, got into an argument about nothing at all, as I recall, one of them asked us to step outside. Bad decision. We escorted them around into an alley.*

"Now you sonsabitches need to git on your plow horses and git the hell outa our town," *Jake explained eloquently.* *"If ya know what's good fer ya,"* *he added.*

"I'm sorry, Jake, but I guess I'm not clear on the 'good for ya' part." *I replied.*

"Stupid," *he scoffed. I didn't think so, and told him that.* *"Really stupid,"* *he corrected himself.*

"Maybe before we let this get out of hand," Charlie piped in congenially, "you boys might want to give us your guns." He smiled. The brothers frowned and looked at each other in utter disbelief. One of them, I forget which, laughed.

"I'll tell you what we're gonna give you," the older one, Carroll, said, his voice with just a tremor of excitement.

"And what would that be?" I asked, shifting my weight to my right side in anticipation.

"This!" Carroll Owens grunted as he pulled his pistol from his belt.

I pushed my weight forward to my left side as I threw a right fist, followed through when I hit him square on the chin, the blow snapping his head back but not off. He dropped his gun and stood legs astraddle, a different kind of tremor coursing through his body. While he staggered and I loaded up, Charlie hit Jake Owens flush on his left ear. Jake dropped like a stone into a pond. Blood quickly appeared on the side of his head.

I hit Carroll again, this time with a combination left cross to his kidney and a right uppercut that was the best one I'd thrown that year. Saliva and blood spewed out of his mouth and nose as his arms flailed back over his head. His feet rose up off the ground and he hit, head first, four feet deeper into the alley where only two of us now stood. I reached down and picked up his pistol, unloaded it, stuck it in the back of my belt. Siringo knelt down at the crumple that was Jake and did the same.

We hauled them to the jail, put them on a train to St. Louis a few days later.

"Hrmph," Will made a disgusted noise that sounded something like that. "Didn't shoot 'em?"

"Didn't shoot 'em," I echoed. "Didn't need to that time. The law wanted them in jail, that was what we went there to do."

"Would you have shot them if they'd pulled their guns?" the boy implored.

"Reckon so," I said. Damn straight, I thought.

"Three aces," he said matter of factly.

"Huh?"

"Three aces," he repeated, and laid his cards on the crate. Sure enough. Damn, I was good, letting him win without even paying attention. Eleven million dollars.

The man's name, it turned out, was Ben Jones, "no relation to the mayor," someone had assured us. He was an apothecary, a druggist from Houston. He'd been in Galveston on some kind of business, Chief Ketchum figured, got caught in the storm and made his way to the Gresham place like the others. No one remembered that he'd come in with anybody else. No one had heard the shot above the storm's bellow. Nobody remembered anything from that night. Hardly blame them. Yes, he had been upstairs, a woman recalled during the interrogations, but she wasn't sure which floor.

As for the redheaded man I had seen peeking down in that moment, he disappeared altogether. We had rounded everyone up as best we could over the next hour. Ketchum – I was glad to see he had survived the storm - made his way eventually to the crime scene. But in the confusion anyone could have just walked right out the front door of the castle, never been noticed.

I didn't have any evidence he was part of the murder anyway, just a notion. That instant did register somewhere in my mind, though: I was fairly certain I would recognize him if I ever saw him again.

As that Sunday morning wore into afternoon, most of us wandered outside to survey what was left of the city. The weather had cleared, a cool breeze - for September - gently stroked the mortally-wounded island, and the hurricane had vanished onto the mainland.

The picture we saw was surreal, a cruel joke played by nature on an otherwise innocent community. A grotesque skyline presented itself, not of buildings but of rubble. The Catholic Church across the street was nothing but brick and wire and shattered, colored glass. Entire rows of homes that had stood along Broadway the morning before had simply evaporated. One set of four or five houses seemed to have just moved from one block to the next, they tilted against one another like dominoes. The streets were piled with the storm's refuse, trees and poles and misshapen concrete boulders, twenty, thirty feet high. Water still ran along makeshift curbs, no more than ankle deep now. For every tree that still stood, leaning at best, fifty had been stomped on like toothpicks. Sand drifted everywhere, sand dunes turning neighborhoods into beachheads.

Here and there people wandered aimlessly, in groups of three or four, huddled together as they would stop in front of pile, peering in delicately as if expecting something awful to leap out at them. Someone in the group would shake a head or point away, and the group would move on to the next stack of debris. A few walked alone, but not many that I could see. A man shuffling along, head down, hands stuffed in his pockets, dejected. A young woman, her hands folded at her waist, bustling along too quickly, frantically, searching. Tears streamed down her face, glistened in the abrupt sunlight. Every several rushed steps she would brush the tears with the back of a hand, resume her folded position, rush along. I saw a small child, nine or ten years of age, I supposed, picking its way through the rubble. She held a piece of a blanket in one hand, her thumb of the other planted firmly in her mouth. She had a perfectly blank expression.

By that Sunday evening - it now seemed like months ago, not six days - the full reality of the horror was sinking in to those of us who had survived the storm. The few of us. One wag in the crowd had suggested that "dozens of folks," as he had put it, may have died. That seemed terrible at the time, incredibly naïve by sundown. The guessing game escalated like a multiplication table: a hundred, no, five hundred a priest had ventured; maybe ten times that. Staggering numbers. Incomprehensible.

Abbie and I joined dozens of others in the digging that day and through the next. A train got through with more rescue workers, but not enough. Never enough. We pulled bodies from the town's wreckage for hours on end, whole, parts, pieces. Loaded them on wheelbarrows and carts, piled a dozen high and deep. Lost count. Lost our senses. Nearly lost our minds.

Some did. A shovel or pick flung to the ground. A primal scream. Running down the street, arms waving in terror, disappearing around a corner. Over and over. Nausea swept over us repeatedly until we paid no attention. The water undrinkable, we downed bottles of ale and whiskey, tore pieces of bread into bites. Little else available.

They told us more bodies had been found closer to the beach. We never went there. Some drifting in from the Gulf where they had been sent by the riptides and undercurrents. Men piling bodies at gunpoint so they wouldn't run away from the disheartening job. One or two shot and killed when they resisted. Barges were pulled around from the bay and loaded with bodies, tugged out into the Gulf and dumped unceremoniously. The next morning, and again on Tuesday, the bodies floated back in, laid along the deteriorating beach. The stench, they said, was unmerciful; the pyres finally a resting place for most.

Will Murney had had an eventful experience in the storm.

"The fellas and I drifted away from you when the wave hit," he explained to Abbie and me on Tuesday afternoon as we sat outside the railway station. "Maybe two or three blocks we rode it hard. Then the water turned on us and the tree just flipped right around and started going the other way! We held on for everything. Right back past the orphanage but I couldn't see you anywhere. I hollered for awhile, but I got tired.

"The water turned all salty and we saw a sand dune go by. I figgered we were heading out into the ocean, and nothing to do about it, either. Just kept holding on. Francis, he fell off one time, but a limb caught him and I pulled him up on my back. It was so dark we couldn't even see ourselves, kept talking just so's we knew we were all three still on. Wind just howled, waves got bigger and bigger. One time turned that tree right straight up like it was planted again.

"Anyhow, after awhile the waves went away and the wind knocked down. We could feel us pushing back to the island. Started seeing piles of stuff, then the tree just slammed - bang! - right into the side of a house somewhere up the island. We figgered it was our chance. I hollered and the fellas jumped down and dived inside the house. Just like that. Water went down. We walked back to town. The other fellas had just turned off when you seen me." Will straightened his shoulders as an exclamation point to his tale. "Some trip, yessir."

Abbie worked that week with a strength beyond anything I'd ever seen. She outdid most of the men when we worked the rubble piles, comforted orphans and widows when the terrible news would come, set up field hospitals all over town, and generally never gave up on getting the city back on its feet. When the only thing she owned – the dress she had on – finally gave out, she boiled water, washed some old rag dresses that had been recovered, and created a wardrobe that still somehow looked spectacular on her.

We found a room in a partially-damaged office building on the Strand, and with some minor furnishings it became our residence. Will Murney stayed at the Gresham house. Abbie and I would finish just after sunset each day, scrape a meal together, and drop exhausted on the makeshift bed where the rest of the world – at least for a time – did not exist. Just the two of us.

Utter exhaustion tempered our lovemaking, but the reserves still held forth long enough each night. Next morning, right at first light, Abbie would nudge me awake, already on her feet and dressing for the day's toil. Enduring.

On Thursday I took up my security job over in Houston at William Marsh Rice's Merchants and Planters Oil Company warehouse. Mr. Rice wired me from New York to see if I was still alive and was anything left of his properties. I returned his message, told him everything on the island was destroyed but I would get over to Houston and survey any damage there. Rice also instructed me to get in touch right away with Captain Baker, his attorney there in Houston. He suggested I go ahead and set up a security watch. It was what he had brought me down there and paid me for in the first place, after all. I wired him back, told him I was on my way.

The warehouse stood on a side rail across the Buffalo Bayou from downtown, next to the German Southern Methodist Church. The Methodist preacher offered me the small room in the basement where Will and I now enjoyed a very bad poker game. I promised to pay some rent while I was there but the preacher said that was all right, he appreciated my being in the neighborhood and would I mind keeping one eye on the church as well and maybe I could even make a service or two on Sundays. I was pretty clear on the first part, not so sure about the last offer. I told him I'd do my best.

Abbie decided to stay on the island for the time being, seeing as how she had plenty of work still to do there. I promised I'd come over as often as I could. She said that would be fine. Will wanted to come see where I was going to be set up, and today was his second visit over. He hadn't found any of his cousins yet, and figured they had died in the storm. He'd be fine.

I tried to see James Baker on Friday but he was out of the office – Baker & Botts law firm – for the day and I would be welcome to come back on Monday morning, the woman who met me at the door had said. I told her my name, what I was doing and where I was staying, said I'd be back Monday. She was polite, though not overwhelmed.

Now it was early Saturday afternoon, a bright, warm day in the humid city. I was out eleven million dollars to my twelve-year-old sidekick, too damn far away from the woman I'd fallen in love with during a hurricane – romance against all odds - but glad to have something concrete to be doing: earning my keep.

When the door to my modest *hacienda* opened and two men appeared from the basement hallway, my gut told me things were getting ready to be somewhat unsettled.

Both were dressed to the nines, dark suits, vests, white shirts, one had a bowler hat and the other a wide-brim. The fellow on my left carried a gutta-percha walking stick but I doubted that he had a limp. He also wore a shiny watch fob, its chain politely dangling across the front of his vest. I imagined he could probably tell time. They stood there in identical stance, legs braced evenly apart, weight shifted to the center, but casually not tense. I hated that.

"Will, why don't you go see if the preacher's made dinner plans," I said in an even voice. I didn't take my eyes off the two visitors.

"Nah, that's all right," he replied in a smart-aleck tone. "I'd druther stay."

"Go on, son," I insisted. "I'll be up directly, soon as these gentlemen have said their business." Will paused, knowing where things were probably headed. Got up on his feet reluctantly, walked to the door. Both men moved their hips imperceptibly to allow room for the boy to pass between them. Will made sure he nudged against both of them anyway. Went up the stairs. The fellow on my right frowned slightly.

"Gentlemen," I offered. Waited. Smiled my most congenial smile. Mr. Friendly.

"Mr. Lincoln?" the bowler hat said, his voice like a hard November rain.

I nodded. At your service, I thought but didn't say. I was still sitting, cross-legged, unfortunate position given the circumstances. Leaping to my feet seemed unwise.

"Mr. Lincoln," Bowler Hat repeated, "you have an item in your possession that belongs to our client. He would be obliged if you would hand it over to us." Obliged.

"And what item would that be?" I honestly inquired. Still ever-pleasant.

"I think you know what we are referring to," he said a little harder. "It would mean nothing to you and our client would be most appreciative." He talked too much: whatever it was just became a lot dearer to me.

"Perhaps your, uhm, client could come himself and we could have a chat about this item." I casually placed both hands against the sides of the crate in front of me.

"That would not be possible," Bowler Hat seemed to be the spokesman of the group; the other fellow looked bored.

"If you could give me a hint about this thing you want, I might be more inclined to continue this conversation."

"A slip of paper, Mr. Lincoln. Of no consequence to you. Meaningless." Right.

"No idea what you're talking about," I said, my brain sifting through the inventory of my meager possessions. Slip of paper? I shrugged.

Bowler Hat never changed expressions. "Come on, Lincoln," his tone seemed a bit unfriendly all of a sudden - was it something I said? "Hand it over. Now."

"Oh, *that* piece of paper," I said with exclamation of suddenly remembering. Still no idea. But this conversation wasn't going to get any better. Using the tone in my voice as an excuse, I pulled up on my knees as if I were going to reach into my pocket for this treasure.

Instead, I gripped the crate, turned my hips to get some balance, and threw it deliberately at a space between the two over-dressed thugs. Cards flew in all directions, like a smoke screen. Well, not much of one. Instinctively the two turned toward the flying box. I followed the crate to my feet and bulldogged into both men with shoulders aimed at their stomachs. I hit Bowler Hat where I aimed but missed the other guy. Bowler Hat gasped as his breath left his lungs. His fancy cane flew off behind him into the shadows. His partner put his hands together in a large fist, raised his arms and slammed the fist down between my shoulder blades, all in one fluid motion. He'd done this before.

As I fell to my knees I pitched into his, buckling them awkwardly. My bad shoulder screamed in pain. He fell nearly on top of me, grimacing. Bowler Hat was getting his breath back. I had about ten more seconds. I arched my back up and over, swinging my right elbow in a wheeling motion down into the middle of the silent man's back. I followed with my left hand, still bandaged from the wrist bone I'd broken in the hurricane, and drove my fist several times into the back of his neck. I was up on top of him now. I grabbed a fistful of hair and pounded his face into the concrete floor. Blood and bone spattered out from under him. I could feel when he let go. So I did.

Two seconds left. I'd underestimated. When I turned to find him, Bowler Hat was in full swing, a left cross catching me on the chin and launching me off his compadre and halfway across the room. I did a very bad somersault but came up on my feet. I shook my head to make the stars go away. Regained my balance. Took a step in his direction.

A loud *whap* echoed into the tiny room like a gunshot. Bowler Hat crumpled into a heap in front of me, unconscious before he hit the ground. I looked past him as he fell. Will Murney stepped into the doorway, the gutta-percha cane in his clutches. He'd used it like a baseball bat, caught the guy flush in the back of his head. The hat had propelled over to my feet. Will had an extra large smirk on his face.

"Nice hit," I said.

"Yeah, thanks."

I rubbed my chin as I walked over and knelt beside Bowler Hat. He seemed to be the better candidate for consciousness, and was already rolling over onto his back, moaning. His partner lay very still, bleeding profusely from several ports. I grabbed some of Bowler's shirt front and pulled his head off the floor. He half-opened his eyes. I bent down into his face. Close.

"You tell your client that I do not have what he wants. And if I did I believe it would now be much more difficult for him to obtain it from me. You tell him to come see me in person if he wants to continue this conversation, and not to send goons. Do you understand the message?" He nodded in a stupid kind of manner, his head lolling.

"Good," I concluded. "Now please take your twin over there and get out of my place." I sat back on my haunches, let him go. He fell back on his cracked skull. Must've hurt. "Goodness knows," I looked around, "it'll take me the rest of the day to clean the place up." Will smiled.

I stood up and backed off, picked up my holster from the cot and pulled the pistol into my hand. It took another full minute for the gentlemen visitors to get their wits about them and two more to stumble up the stairs. Then they were gone.

"What're they after, Cale?" Will asked, tossing his lethal weapon to the floor.

"Dunno," I replied. But I did know. It had come to me in the midst of the head-pounding. I knew what they were after. And I knew where it was. What I didn't know was what was on that piece of paper and why anyone would want it.

"I'm going back to Galveston to see Abbie," I said. "Wanna come?"

12

—◦◦◦◦◦—

We made the 1:30 train and were in Galveston before mid-afternoon. Will took off to find his buddies, said he'd see me next week. I said okay, and thanked him again for his help. No problem, he called over his shoulder as he headed down the street.

I found Abbie a block from the apartment, outside on a street corner that had been cleared away for a makeshift communications center. Someone had pulled a rickety table and some chairs from a nearby building and set them out on the corner. Papers were strewn across the table, with gravel as paperweights in the island breeze. I glanced at the papers as I rounded the end of the table: lists of names. Missing, probably dead.

Abbie the Angel and I embraced and held it for a very long time, maybe half of what I needed. I kissed her deeply, probably embarrassing the neighbors, but she drew back when I winced. My chin hurt. She looked at me curiously, then furrowed her eyebrows. I held both her hands in front of me while I told her what had happened. She shook her head with alarm.

"I need to get back to the room, Abbie. I need those pants I was wearing in the storm."

"I washed them, Cale," she said matter-of-factly. I frowned.

"Did you find anything in the pockets?" She mulled over that for a moment.

"Yes." She frowned, concentrating. It had been a week. "Two bullets. Some coins, dollars I think. Handkerchief, very dirty," she added. "A prescription. And - that's all." She raised her eyebrows, hoping she had mentioned the something I needed. Nothing rang a bell -

"A prescription?" I blurted. "On a piece of paper?" I added, rather stupidly. No dear, it was on one of the bullets.

"A prescription," she said again, simply, with a short nod of her head.

"Do you remember what was on it?"

"No. I'm sorry."

"No, no, that's all right. Why should you? Did you throw it away?"

"Of course not," she said, a bit hurt. "I put all of those items in a pouch. They are in a dresser drawer." I pulled her to me, kissed her fully on the mouth, deeper, thought briefly about holding that position until, well, Christmas perhaps. Decided I had better finish whatever had been started with that piece of paper. Pulled back a fraction.

"Let's go back to the house," I whispered.

"I have work to do here, Cale," she argued. I smiled my very best smile, turned down just a bit from the chin bruise. She relented. "Oh, all right. But I must get back to work soon." We fell into step. Debonair, I thought to myself. Killer smile.

I took the last steps at a bound in anticipation of at least two things happening in the next few moments. Both came true. In the second drawer of the remnants of a dresser we had picked up I found the small beige pouch, its string neatly tied in a bow. I pulled on the string and emptied its contents onto the top of the dresser. The bullets clanked and one spun onto the floor. The handkerchief remained filthy. The piece of paper was wadded and stained from the incessant wet of the storm. I unfolded it as carefully as if it was a piece of evidence for a crime that had been committed. The ink had run in several places but there were only two words on the small sheet, across the middle: MERCURY TABLETS. At the bottom the pharmacist's scribbled signature: *Ben Jones*, the man who had been shot and killed inside Gresham's home last Sunday morning. What in the world it meant I still had no idea. But whoever the goons' client was, he wanted this prescription badly. And not, I surmised, for his health.

"What does it mean, Cale?" Abbie asked as she sidled up to my side, peering over my shoulder at the clue. Clue to what? The murder? I shook my head.

"I don't know yet, Abbie," I said evenly. "But I guess I'm going to find out, one way or the other."

"You mean your visitors today?"

"Yes. I suppose they will return, or ten more like them. Whoever sent them wants this little piece of paper very badly."

"What will you do if they come again?" She put her hand on my arm. I patted it.

"Same thing, I guess. Discourage them. Maybe let them take me to their employer."

"Which would, of course, put you in extreme danger."

"It would put me nearer the truth of whatever is going on here."

"They might have guns next time."

"They would need a lot of them to stop me."

"Are you trying to sound brave just to keep me from being afraid?"

"No, I try to sound this way all the time."

"Yes, you usually do." Abbie gripped my arm tighter with each comment.

"I would need some encouragement, however, in order to remain brave in the face of such bad men." She pulled at my arm, stepped back toward the bed.

"I believe encouragement is my role." I followed her to the bed. No argument there.

An hour later we were headed back to the street. I was very much encouraged. I hated to leave Abbie on the island, but I needed to get back to the warehouse and that was the last place I wanted her for the time being. I made the 6:00 train back to Houston, had supper at the Rice Hotel on my way through town, and was walking along Clark Street in front of the church by dark. I sported a new cane left behind by my attacker. Dashing look, that.

Clark Street, which went in front of the warehouse, and Roanoke met just where a side rail track veered off through the warehouse itself and on out to Baron Avenue, crossing St. Charles on its way. St. Charles, running east and west and parallel to the bayou six blocks away, actually deadended in the middle of Rice's warehouse. The Merchants & Planters Oil building took up an entire city block.

It had been damaged by the storm, a corner of the roof caved in, some of the roof itself long gone, and a six foot pile of bricks on the ground below. Windows on the north side - Baron Avenue - had broken. The remainder of the thirty-foot high edifice was intact. I had looked over nearly every square foot of the place in the last two days, and boarded up the shattered windows on the north wall. Inside the warehouse was practically empty. Several old wagons lay about, some piles of used equipment here and there, a stack of cotton bales and assorted burlap sacks, the tracks that ran through the southeast corner hosted one lonesome tow car sitting idle. Ropes and tongs and pulleys hung from rafters and beams, with several rakes and shovels pinned against the walls. There were two main entrances, double-wide barn-size doors where the tracks entered and exited; a regular size door stood on each of the four walls, none centered. More toward each corner. Padlocks served as discouragers on all four doors plus the two train entries which also sported huge chains across their fronts. I was the other discouragement, should anyone have wanted to break in and steal a rake.

When they came at me, they weren't after a rake.

There were four of them this time, hidden in the shadows at the base of the building in two groups. As I passed the rail entry on Clark Street two of them stepped out from behind at the same moment their two cohorts stepped in front. I turned my body slightly so my back was more or less to the wall of the building. I could see the four of them as they ambled closer on my left and right. I held the cane in front of me, both hands resting lightly on its crown. Casual look, very good on me.

"Gentlemen," I began what was likely going to be a brief conversation. "A beautiful evening."

One of the two on my right, the tallest of the four, took an additional step in my direction. Ten feet away. He was dressed in work clothes, cotton and denim, brown, boots, no hat. The others in similar outfits. The nearest light, a street lamp some sixty feet up Clark, cast odd shadows on all of us as we stood there.

"Ya know why we're here, mister," the spokesman said roughly. "Give us that goddamned piece of paper."

"Oh," I said, apparently surprised and delighted. "You must know the two gentlemen who visited me earlier today." I smiled. The spokesman turned to his pal and frowned. Back to me.

"Stupid sonuvabitch," he offered.

"Maybe so," I replied. "What difference do you suppose that might make here?"

"'Cuz when we beat the crap outa you, you're gonna be sorry you didn't come through. That's what." He drew his shoulders back. The other three took a step in tandem toward me. The two on my left each held what looked like billy clubs; the other two were empty-handed for the moment. I calculated the odds on several things that could happen next.

"I'm sorry you feel that way," I finally said, still congenial. "I thought we had something going here between us."

"Shuddup with the wisecracks," Spokesman blurted. "Give it over, if ya know what's good for ya." All of the fellas I'd met today seemed to have graduated from the same school of elocution.

"If I had what you wanted, you dumb bastard," I was wearying of the gabbing, "you'd play hell getting it from me. But I don't," I lied: the slip of paper was nestled in my pocket as we spoke.

"What'd you call me?" the one with a voice said, taking another step in my direction.

"If you'll just come a bit closer, I'd be pleased to whisper it in your ear."

"Why, you -" he started. I took one long stride right at him, pulling the cane up in my right hand in the same motion. I swung it backhanded with the force of my legs behind it, striking him across the throat. He made a loud gurgling sound and a grunt at the same time, his head snapped forward and then back in an instant, and he fell on his back and didn't move again.

I was no longer paying attention to him, though. I stepped right past him and headed for his nearest partner, who in those three seconds had reached for a pistol stuck in his belt at his back. His head was down at an angle as he grabbed for it. I followed through with the cane stroke that had felled his buddy. The metallic tip of the walking stick glanced across his right cheek and the bridge of his nose. Blood spurted out in front of him as his head whipped with the blow. He performed an ungainly pirouette into the brick wall, slamming face first.

I didn't bother to look behind me. I was fairly certain the other two thugs had not been watching this without reacting. I had maybe fifteen feet on them and was already heading away at a trot, taking a short leap over the downed man on my way into some shadows that ran against the building.

I could hear their steps on the cobblestone street as we ran. They weren't gaining, nor falling impossibly behind. I took the turn at the corner of the building, onto Baron Avenue, and picked up speed. It was pitch black on the north side of the warehouse, but my followers were close enough to keep me more or less in sight.

My thoughts raced as I did. I had two more doors to pass if I continued around the building: both would be padlocked. Taking off into the neighborhood was a possibility, but I knew very little about what was out there. My one chance, other than stopping and facing them - my least favorite option, was the rail door on the east side. Though chained and locked, it had some give in it, I remembered, maybe enough for a man to wedge through. Maybe not.

I turned at the northeast corner of the warehouse I was supposed to be guarding, picked up speed and headed for the wide double doors. I had a fifteen step lead. I reached the doors and threw my shoulder at the crack where they met. The chain just above my head rattled in defiance. The padlock swung up and out, and back against the door. The door gave as my momentum pushed against it. Six inches, then a foot, the crack widened. I had no second chance at this. Turned sideways, head first with a knee shoved hard against the door, the chain sprang tight but I was through an instant later, tumbling inside the dark recesses onto the warehouse floor. The rail doors rattled and shook behind me.

If I could get through, so could my two remaining assailants. I got to my feet, scrambling deeper into the dark building. I could hear them behind me, working against the massive doors. They were nearly inside. I tripped on one of the rails that coursed through the building, lost my balance, and threw my hands in front of me as I fell. I managed to keep some balance and was back on my feet a moment later.

I looked over my shoulder for the first time since the race began. I could barely make out the two men, dim shadows, phantoms, poking along much more carefully than me. Their clubs were raised above their heads in readiness. They walked six feet apart, but right at me, whether they knew it or not.

I pulled my pistol from its holster as I wheeled around and stopped. Feet planted, knees slightly bent, in a crouch, balanced. I pointed the gun with arms extended, one hand wrapped around the other at the butt of the .44. I pulled the trigger twice - being economical - once at the shadow to my left, then a slight turn and at the other guy. At twenty-five feet and in the dark my aim was no more than general. The first fellow shouted some incoherent "ugh" and disappeared from my marginal view. The second one also vanished but it looked in that instant that he was diving for cover, not falling from injury.

It got very quiet in Mr. Rice's Merchants & Planters warehouse. I kept my gun pointed out in front of me, and held my breath. Cocked one ear with a turn of my chin, listening for any movement, any target. Not a sound. The one I'd probably shot wasn't making any noise; the one who had dived to safety was still as a stone. Likely doing the same thing I was. Listening. Waiting.

I can hold my breath under water for an impressively long time. But the run halfway around the building and the struggles along the way had sapped my lungs. I exhaled, inhaled as silently as I could. Nothing. Lowered my gun to a 45 degree angle. Took another breath.

The shot rang out like the Liberty Bell in Philly, its echo bouncing off the walls. I heard that terrible whistling sound at my left ear - I'd been that close before. The bullet whizzed by me before I could move a muscle, shattered itself against something off behind in the shadows.

I caught the brief flare from the other guy's pistol, pulled my gun up and shot where it had been one second before. I heard my bullet bang against a far wall. It must have hit some metal, because it pinged twice more in the darkness. I'd missed, too.

I heard movement off to my right, a shuffling sound like someone crawling along a dirt floor. I backed up slowly, my gun still pointed at the noise, squinting into the shadows for any movement that might become a target. I decided not to shoot aimlessly; and I decided not to worry about the first guy who I was pretty sure I had hit. One at a time.

As I reached what I considered to be the center of the warehouse, I turned behind a wooden column that rose to the ceiling beams for support. I knelt down, placed my left arm against the column to brace myself, and extended the pistol with both hands. And I waited. Ten seconds. Thirty. Probably a minute, although by then it seemed like a couple of days had gone by. Twice I heard the barest noise, the shuffling of someone on hands and knees, perhaps. Still off to my right, closer each time. I counted to ten, took a deep breath, and let it out slowly.

A scuffling sound twelve feet to my right. I turned the gun and fired three times in rapid succession. I heard a clanking noise - a gun falling to the floor. I came to my feet and raced directly at the sound, covering the distance in several strides, gun still pointed.

He hit me right below my knees and I went down in a terrible somersault, rolled right by him. Saw the billy club following through from its blow. Pain arched up through my legs and up my spine. I gritted my teeth as I rolled on my tender shoulder. My gun skittered away into the darkness.

He was running. I could hear him slipping, falling, scrambling to his feet, the sound moving away from me back toward the entry. I rubbed my shins, shook my head to clear it as I came to my feet. Wobbly. Back down on hands and knees looking for my gun. Hands full of dirt and straw, no gun. He was getting away. I went after him.

Bone against metal. A really ugly *thump* somewhere ahead of me. A noise like a sack of potatoes hitting the ground. A small squeal from above, cable on a pulley somewhere in the rafters. Five more strides. Slowing as I reached the vicinity of the noises. Now quiet.

He was laying on the ground face down, legs and arms at awkward angles, motionless. As I reached his side and bent down for a closer look, I heard something swing just inches above my head. I crooked my neck and looked up. The huge hook had missed me by a whisker. My unconscious pal here had run full tilt into it, causing it to sway. I put my fingers against his neck. Faint pulse. Hardly breathing. Probably a skull in less than pristine condition. I noticed the billy club laying two feet away. Picked it up.

Smelled the smoke.

13

It quickly enveloped the warehouse, black cloud against black shadows. I headed for the double doors where I'd come in moments earlier, having a general idea where they might be. The temperature rose as I hurried. I stumbled - again - on the tracks, kept my balance and reached out for the doors. I hadn't missed my mark but by a few feet. I felt my way until my fingers grasped the edge of the doors, the crack where I had pushed through. I leaned my shoulder hard against the spot. Nothing gave. Not even an inch. Interesting. I pushed again. Tried to wedge my foot at the bottom. No play. The smoke roiled around me. I was blinking, my eyes starting to water. I took short, shallow breaths, kept pushing against the doors. No give. My hands moved up along the tiny crack until they were at eye level. I felt steel through the opening on the other side. A metal bar of some sort. Wedged down against the doors, my only avenue of escape. Someone on the outside had barred my one route to safety.

I turned, my back against the doors. Tried to peer through the dense smoke. Considered my options. That didn't take very long.

I pushed off into the cloud, taking one deep breath as I moved. I squinted as I walked out into the warehouse. Directly, more or less, across the floor was the other railway entrance to the building. The chances of it being barred shut were fairly good, but I had little other chance. Maybe my pursuer - whoever it was - had made a mistake. Not likely. Had to try.

Groping through the smoke, the heat beginning to tell. Off to my right I saw the flames for the first time, rising up the north wall as they caught on straw and board and bales. A single line of fire climbed up a rope in the distance, like a cobra coming up out of its basket. The sound of the fire increased. I coughed, brought a handkerchief up to my mouth and nose. Kept walking steadily, not hurrying. No tripping this time. No time.

I bumped into the west wall. Threw my hands up against it, feeling my way along, left, then back to the right. Was I at the door? Where would it give way? Couldn't stop coughing. Eyes shut tight against the acrid smoke. Groping. Blind. On my knees.

The smoke rose up from ten miles distant, roiling into the sky like an Arapaho signal. Prairie fires could not sneak up on a man in the Montana hills: you could see 'em coming for miles. What you couldn't do is outrun them. I turned my mount to the southeast, directly away from where the fire raced, urged him on.

I had been in the area for three months, barely enough to know my way around. No caves, no box canyons. But a wide river basin curled along less than two miles from where I now rode. The Little Big Horn, they called it. Winding through the valleys, dividing and reuniting, five hundred feet wide in places, never very deep except in the occasional pools that had formed in the gullies.

I rode hard, but the fire seemed to be catching up. I looked over my shoulder every few minutes. The white smoke billowed like a summer cloud high into the sky. The flames would consume everything in their path, a mile wide and maybe twenty miles long before playing out. I had no intention of being part of its meal.

I made a rise and looked down the slope. The Little Big Horn spread out in front of me, still a thousand yards away, twisting its way out of Montana country and onto the plains. I stopped long enough to turn in the saddle and gauge the fire that was chasing me. I would make the river.

I paused, let my horse take a breather. The last run would be downhill, steep but not impossible. Sat back on my haunches. Looked around me.

I was on the crest of one of several small hills that rose up to create the myriad valleys here. I could see the tops of the others in each direction. I looked down at the ground where my mount now grazed on the knee-high prairie grass. What at first looked like piles of strange, too-white rocks, partially hidden in the grass, now began to take on familiar shapes and patterns: bones, dozens of them strewn about here. Cattle? Buffalo? Too small for that.

A rib cage stuck its empty chest out off to my left. I leaned far over in the saddle for a better look. A man's skull stared back at me, eye sockets black-empty, looking past me to some other world somewhere. A crooked fissure made its way across the top of the skull, finishing where a forehead had once had skin and hair.

I came up straight in the saddle, popped the reins at the same time. My mount jumped into his gait, headed for the river bottom. The smoke drifted now right above us.

I blinked my eyes open. The smoke was thick like soup. I couldn't catch my breath. I was on my hands and knees, my left side leaning against the wall of the warehouse. Had to get to my feet. Pushed up. A knee buckled, held. My back slid against the wood. Fire in every direction, tongues of it lapping up higher into the rafters. A barrel of something exploded off in the blackness, fireworks peeked through.

I slid to my left, my left hand groping its way along the wall. Ten feet. Ten more. A window sill struck my upper arm, its corner sticking me like a poker. I swung my right arm, extended out from my body, in a long arc like a huge uppercut. My fist smashed through glass, the shattering sound above the din of the fire around me. Air whooshed out of the opening into the night air outside. I turned and gripped the sill with both hands, the right one stinging as the glass shards cut bloody lines across the tops of my fingers and my wrist. I would worry over that later.

Pulled myself up, leaned forward through the opening, remnants of the window glass slicing into my shirt. Pushed with my soles, up, out falling forward, a swing of my hips and my hands made contact with Clark Street brick. I turned the leap into a somersault, rolled over onto my rear. Balanced. Shook my head to clear it. The roaring behind me increased, a blue-yellow flame licking at the window where I'd been five seconds before.

There was smoke outside, too, but dissipating as it reached in all directions across the warehouse district. I jumped to my feet, bent into a crouch. I wasn't likely out of danger yet. Whoever had barred the doors, the same one who had sent the goons, wanted me dead. Maybe figured I was burned up. Maybe not.

I saw him down the street. He was sitting in a wagon that was facing away, reins in his hand, twisted around to look in my direction. He caught my eye at the same instant.

The streetlight over his head, winning its battle of light against the darkness of the spreading smoke, illuminated the shock of red hair. Two instant glances a week apart, but no doubt in my mind.

Without thinking, an understatement considering the condition I was in, I sprinted for the wagon. No gun, no weapon of any kind, bleeding, hacking the smoke out of my lungs as I ran, my rage took over. I would just tear his head off his shoulders with my bare hands.

He apparently understood, thought ill of the scenario in my mind, turned away from me and cracked the reins on the back of the horse in front of him. The wagon jolted to a start and picked up speed, heading down Clark Street, crossing Roanoke and racing past the church. I kept up my pursuit, running beyond measure, adrenalin pumping my legs.

The wagon turned abruptly at Davis Street, careening onto its left wheels as it made the intersection at full speed. I cut across Clark and ran alongside the buildings, my angle bringing me closer to my prey. I leaned as I turned right onto Davis. The wagon was a half block ahead and now gaining distance again.

The warehouse fire was now just a memory. The only thing that mattered was the man in that wagon. The only thing in my life at that moment.

He made Hill Street while still in view, although I was losing ground. His left turn there meant only one thing: he was headed across the bayou into the city. Once he got into the Houston streets I would lose him. Tonight I would not let that happen.

I summoned additional speed from somewhere deep in my anger, crossing Davis and onto Hill, cutting corners brushing against buildings. As I came to the narrow bridge that spanned Buffalo Bayou I spotted two men off to the left, their heads together, talking. I decided they were of no importance or use to me, headed onto the bridge. The wagon was out of sight, having clambered across nearly a minute ahead of me now.

As I came to south end of the bridge, the murky waters beneath me wallowing about with no real purpose, I slowed to a jog, becoming more cautious, trying to see through the darkness. The lights of the town's street lamps were still too distant to do me any good. I could make out silhouettes, but little else. The streets would likely be emptying at this time of night, allowing me to maybe hear the escaping wagon even if I couldn't see it.

Wouldn't be hearing it, though. It lay there in a ditch to my left, caromed over at a steep angle, its right wheels flung into the night air, the rear wheel just spinning down to a stop as I reached it. I walked carefully to its side, ready for the redheaded man to leap out at me. Hoping he would. A second, distant choice would be to find him underneath the wagon, pinned and dead. Neither happened. The horse had cut loose from the axle and stood fifty feet ahead in the ditch, head down looking for a morsel of grass or thistle. No bodies. No sign.

He had a minute's head start on foot. Maybe injured, slowed. If he had run on down the street I believe I would have seen him already. Or I would have lost him already. Off to the right the road sloped severely back into the bayou - not a good alternative for a man trying to escape unless he planned on drowning to elude me.

On the left was the city cemetery. A wire fence, chest high, ran along the other side of the ditch where I stood, sixty yards in each direction. In the center, not thirty feet away, was the gate, a wrought iron arch over it to encourage a somber attitude upon entering, I supposed. I didn't have a lot of time to change attitude, so I went in with the one that brought me there.

If the darkness could deepen, it did as I passed the gate and stepped inside the graveyard. Gray headstones stood at different angles of attention as far as I could see, maybe fifty feet. I had passed the cemetery several times over the last few days, but had only a bare memory of how large it might be, how far back into the night it went.

I stood quietly, not breathing, listening for a sound, any sound. Of a live human being with red hair would be my preference. Or just a live human being. Silence. The eerie kind.

I took several steps forward, found myself on a wide path that seemed to divide the graves into sections. Trees stood sporadically at the edge of my night vision. Behind a tree, crouched behind a tombstone, lying in a dug out grave: too many hiding places. Little alternative but to keep looking. Each step as silent as I could make it. No twigs, no gravel, no mistakes. Still unarmed, I would be dangerous if I had the chance to get to this guy. Why was I a target? Was it the prescription that the dead man, Jones, had had in his pocket, now mine? And what about it if it was? Mercury tablets? How dangerous, how important could that be? Important enough to kill for? Besides, I concluded my musings as I stalked the path, I was damn tired of getting beaten up. Enough.

A fluttering sound, loud flapping just to my right, startling me to attention. I turned my hips, still in a crouch, arms extended and ready for the attack. Come on. The owl loomed up in front of me and effortlessly flew over, missing my head by only inches. I dropped my head instinctively, threw one hand into the air to deflect the attack that never came. I watched as the wide wingspan vanished back into the darkness. Damn bird.

The blow caught me just below my ribs, but flush. I bent over at the waist in pain, air rushing out of my lungs. Fell back, stumbling to keep my balance. Failing that I fell flat on my back, my head missing the edge of a gravestone by less than a foot. I grabbed at the stone to pull myself up, managed it awkwardly, still no breath. I heard something drop just in front of me, but I was paralyzed by the blow and couldn't move for maybe ten seconds.

When I did I had lost him. The limb he had hit me with lay at my feet, a souvenir. I had just glanced his movement, running back out the gate, to his left toward the city. He would disappear there. For now. Not forever. Another time, Red. I promise.

Damn bird.

14

September 17, 1900

Mr. William Marsh Rice

Park Avenue, New York City

Mr. Rice: Fire in Warehouse 15 Sept STOP Damage serious STOP Two dead STOP Contacting Baker STOP Await Instructions STOP Lincoln

The day before I sent the Good News telegram to my employer, sure to thrill him and want me to be his security chief forever, I spent the morning in the Houston sheriff's office at the jailhouse. I handed over the prescription after a lengthy explanation of the murder on Galveston Island, and answered a million questions or so regarding the warehouse fire. And about those two charred bodies inside. I did a lot of less than helpful shrugging, some because I honestly had no idea who they were, some because I knew why they were there but thought I would keep that to myself for now. I did not offer any connection between the two incidents, and it wasn't brought up. The sheriff let me go, told me not to leave Houston for the time being, and suggested I get a place there rather than returning to Galveston. The fact that I nominally was working for Mr. Rice helped some, and that I had used Captain Baker's name as well.

Now, two days later, I was sitting in James Baker's office, having decided I should visit with him before the authorities found out I didn't in fact know the man. One step ahead.

Captain James Baker, of Baker & Botts Law Firm Inc. of Houston, was an impressive character from the get-go. Almost as tall as me, wide shouldered and a pretty hefty girth, he didn't hint of anything flabby or lazy. Confidence poured out of him, a self-assurance that had no ego or vanity to it: he was what he believed he was. That was good enough for me. His office was likewise unassuming, parts of it well-organized and neat, other stacks – probably the active cases – less self-assured. I could have worked there. I don't recall being invited to, however.

Baker spoke with an inner strength, not a loud voice but one with authority. Make that two things I liked about him. "Heard back from Mr. Rice yet?" he was asking. I shook my head. He continued, "You will. He'll let you have it when he hears about the warehouse, even though it wasn't your fault. He's just that way. Brusk, but fair."

"I can handle both of those," I remarked. "Tell me more about him."

"An old buzzard, for one," Baker began, settling back in his chair. He looked toward the ceiling and thought out loud. "Millionaire. Earned every penny of it. Been making money since before the war." The one between the states, I assumed. "Railroads, property, investments all over the country. Spends most of his time in New York City nowadays, travels back to Texas some. The warehouse is nothing but penny ante stuff for him – no offense –"

"None taken."

" – but he'll treat it like it was the biggest thing he owned. Might come down to see for himself." Baker paused. "Might not. He's been sick lately, frail. Must be in his nineties, I suppose. Used to make that trip from New York every three, four months sometimes.

"Not much anymore, though," Baker sat back up and looked more or less in my direction. "His second wife died over three years ago now, terrible thing. She was from the Midwest, never did like coming to Texas, maybe to Galveston once in awhile. Her family got all upset about one thing or another when she got sick, tried to get more of the old man's money after she died. I've been fighting them in court ever since. Winning, mostly. It's not over yet. I was just looking back over the will the other day, matter of fact." He frowned. Hard. Quiet for a moment.

"What's the stumbling block?" I interrupted his pause.

"Institute," Baker said. "Mr. Rice put some money back to build a research university here in Houston. Couple hundred thousand dollars. Family's fighting over it." He shrugged. "We'll be all right."

"Wouldn't bet against you," I replied, because I wouldn't.

"So, what's your next move?" he asked, changing the subject.

"Don't know exactly. I'll wait to see if I still have the job. If I do, I'll take care of the inventory of what survived the fire. If not, I'll go looking for the guy who came after me."

"Hope you do both," Baker said. "Don't know what he has going, but it's trouble. And we don't need any of that. If it has anything to do with Mr. Rice, well, that's where I come in." He paused. "I hope you stay on. We could work on this one together."

"Fine by me," I agreed. "Could use another pair of legs to track the guy down. Don't know my way around Houston yet, sure could use the help."

"You'll have it, Mr. Lincoln."

"Cale."

"Cale. Any word on the dead men, or the others who roughed you up?" Painful memory.

"Nope. I'll find out, though."

"Yeah, you Pinkerton men get kind of wound up on your investigations, don't you?"

"Wound up like a top," I replied.

"Well, good luck on that. You stay in touch. When you hear from Mr. Rice you let me know. I've sent him my own message, told him you and I would work together on this. That all right with you?"

I stood up. "Looking forward to it, Cap'n." He stood and we shook hands across the desk. "Take care," I said over my shoulder on the way out the door.

"You're probably the one who needs to do that," he called after me. No kidding.

Thursday, September 20. Galveston. Spent the day with Abbie and Will. Spent the night with Abbie. It had been twelve horrible days since the storm destroyed the island city. The full truth was beginning to bob to the surface for the first time. The numbers would reach far beyond the original estimates, far beyond the hundreds, gruesomely beyond all reality. Someone had used the number three thousand. Impossible.

Volunteers poured into the area, outnumbering the residents who had survived and stayed on the island to rebuild. Thomas Edison had come with a photography crew and left with the horror on film to show the rest of the world. I had run across Edison's people in Cuba two years earlier.

Funeral pyres still burned in parts of the city, especially out toward the beach and west down the island. Bodies, animals, parts of buildings, all went up in purifying flames. The stench remained behind despite all efforts. And the memories.

Abbie and I patrolled the streets for hours, lending a helping hand wherever we could. We moved piles of rubble, pulled bodies from beneath, gave directions to rescue workers, whatever helped. She never seemed to tire. Relentless, unkempt, beautiful. She stayed a step ahead of me most of the day, and had more than enough to keep me busy in the night when we were finally alone. Friday morning, back to the slowly clearing streets.

Captain Baker wanted me to move into Houston and suggested the Rice Hotel, aptly, as a temporary residence. I persuaded Abbie to come with me, promising her I would get her back and forth to the Galveston scene whenever she wanted, convincing her she needed to get away from it whenever possible. She gave in. We moved our meager possessions by train to downtown Houston late Friday afternoon.

We also said goodbye to Will Murney. He had become a part of our little makeshift family for those hectic two weeks, but now distant cousins had come for him and he took off one day. I think he was headed to Ohio. He had mixed feelings about all of it, but his sense of adventure sent him on. Good boy. He'd grown up that night. He'd be fine. He reminded me of me.

I buried her out in the middle of a thicket, overgrown with briar where only a small deer trail wound its way through. I scratched and bled all over as I carried her to that place. She was more than I could manage, dead weight, but I would not be denied this task of burying her right, myself. And where no one would ever bother her again.

I dug the grave with my bare hands and a wide limb, deep enough for me to stand with the surface at my eye level. Four and a half feet, maybe less. I had stolen an army blanket I found hanging from a line at the edge of town, wrapped her in it. Most of her dress and slips had been torn away when they killed her. Her shoes long since gone. A blue ribbon still clung to a braid in her hair. I left it there.

I tried to arrange her body neatly, but the grave was small at the bottom. I'd given out. I crawled out and laid down on my back for an hour, watching billowy clouds pass overhead. Even they didn't know I was there. Then I stood up, rubbed the dirt from my hands onto my britches as best I could, and stared down into the pit. I couldn't think of anything I should say. So I just cried. No sobbing. No noise. Just let the tears go. Never had anymore after that. All cried out.

I shoveled the dirt onto her until the pile on the ground was mostly gone. There were some rocks laying about and I made a little tower of them, stood the digging limb in them, like a headstone I guess. Didn't say anything on it. I knew. That was enough.

"Cale," Abbie's soft voice right at my ear, her breath awash against my cheek.

15

Monday. September 23. Late afternoon.

I was sprawled across the ornate loveseat that held its own against the far wall of the hotel room. Lavender. Not my color. My legs were comfortably thrust out, one to the floor, the other draped over the arm. My head nestled back against a throw pillow, also purplish, as I dozed. I was aware of the small world around me but not altogether interested in doing anything with it. Too comfortable.

Scrunched and wedged and curled in and around my lap, Abbie slept fitfully, making tiny mewing noises that sounded like a kitten caught in a burlap bag but not particularly upset about it. A tousled blanket more or less covered both of us. An early afternoon of lovemaking had swept us from the bed to the lush carpet and finally onto the loveseat, where we now enjoyed the moments after. I brushed her hair with my hand absent-mindedly, and she stirred. Twisted her shoulders a few inches, pulled her hands up under her chin, didn't wake. I loved her scent. Ours.

The knock on the door was fervent, rapid but not loud. Loud enough to jolt me from the reverie. Abbie moaned. The girl could sleep. I managed to extricate myself from our wrap, pulling up and over the other arm, letting her head down gently on the pillow I now gave up. She curled again, the blanket finding the spaces and curves of her body. I hated walking away from that. I grabbed my pants from the floor and pulled them on as I shuffled across the room. The knocking ratatat-tatted once more before I could get there. I glanced at my revolver hanging from its holster on the back of the door: close enough should my guest be trouble.

Wasn't trouble. Not yet anyway. A boy, maybe eight or nine, stood there in the hall. He had a bright expression on his face, a cap in his hands. He looked right up at me, craning his neck but not adjusting his cheery smile. I smiled back.

"Mr. Lincoln?" I nodded. He took a short breath, grimaced as if remembering the message word for word which he now repeated. "Captain Baker requests your presence in his office." Paused. "Right away, sir." I frowned. He did, too. I looked over my shoulder at Abbie. Back at the boy.

"Thank you, son," I said in a whisper. I reached into my pants pocket and retrieved a coin. Flipped it in his direction. He grasped it and had it in his cap all in one motion, never looked away from me. "Please tell Captain Baker I will be there in thirty minutes."

"Yessir," he replied smartly. Doffed his cap, the coin now resting on his head I supposed, turned on a heel and started away. Took two steps, then broke into a dead run down the hall for the stairway.

I was sitting in Baker's law office thirty minutes later. The Gibbs Building, where Baker & Botts officed, stood at a busy downtown corner like a monarch looking over his realm. The spiral turret capped the several story building like a crown. From his window Baker could watch Houston grow right before his eyes. Now his eyes were focused on two telegrams that he held, one in each hand. He pored over them, again, as I sat and waited. He had barely acknowledged my arrival or my presence in the last five minutes. I didn't mind. Something was wrong. I waited.

"I need you to go to New York with me," he said in a steady tone, his eyes still on the messages.

"All right."

"Tonight."

"All right."

"Do you want to know why?"

"You'll tell me when you're ready."

"Here's why." He handed me one of the telegrams, the one in his left hand. I pulled up from the chair to reach across for it, settled back. He stared at the second one while I read the first:

CAPTAIN JAMES BAKER

HOUSTON, TEXAS

SEPTEMBER 23, 1900

2:00 P.M.

    MR. RICE DIED 8 O'CLOCK LAST NIGHT UNDER CARE OF PHYSICIAN. DEATH CERTIFICATE OLD AGE, WEAK HEART, DIARAHUE. LEFT INSTRUCTIONS TO BE INTERRED AT MILWAUKEE WITH WIFE. FUNERAL TEN A.M. TO-MORROW, AT 500 MADISON AVENUE. WHEN WILL YOU COME?

C. F. JONES

So the old man was dead. I hadn't known him much, but I liked his abrupt style, straightforward way. He had seemed pretty frail to me the year before, but his mind was still sharp then. He had responded quickly, alertly, to every comment thrown his way. Or ignored the ones not worth his time. I liked that, too.

I read the telegram over once more, looked up at Baker. His eyes were still down. "Too bad," I said simply. Baker barely nodded. Frowned. A minute went by. I waited. Put the telegram back on the desk. Baker looked up, right at me, his eyes a little too wide open, teeth gritted. Handed me the second telegram. I accepted it without taking my eyes from his. Something else. I looked down. Read:

CAPTAIN JAMES BAKER
HOUSTON, TEXAS
SEPTEMBER 23, 1900
3:00 P.M.

JONES TELEPHONED THIS MORNING MR. RICE DIED LAST NIGHT. A LAWYER HERE PRESENTED DRAFT FOR LARGE AMOUNT AND ASSIGNMENT TO HIMSELF OF ALL SECURITIES AND MONEYS IN OUR HANDS.

I looked up at Baker. His eyes gleamed with a kind of determined excitement. Raised his eyebrows in the direction of the telegram. I read the rest of it:

HE INFORMED US FUNERAL TOMORROW BODY TO BE CREMATED. HAVE CONSULTED BOWERS

AND SANDS LAWYERS THIRTY ONE NASSAU STREET. THINK YOU SHOULD HAVE THEM REPRESENT YOU AT ONCE. WE HAVE SEEN THEM. ANSWER THEM AND US INSTANTLY.

I looked up again. Burial? Cremated? Instantly?

WIRE BOWERS AND SANDS AUTHORITY FROM SOME RELATIVE ABOUT DISPOSITION OF BODY.

At the bottom of the telegram was the address of the law office in New York City. The message was signed "S. M. Swenson and Sons."

I held the paper for a time, mulling it over. Odd. The old man dead. His lawyer there at the bank first thing in the morning, taking money out for himself. Some question about authority. Could be coincidence. Easily explained. I knew better.

"When do we leave?" I asked without looking up.

"Three hours. Meet you at the station." I left.

Part Three

New York City

16

"When will you return?" Abbie sat quietly on the edge of the bed, fingering a blue ribbon she had just pulled from her hair. Her eyes stared right through me.

"Don't know. As soon as I can." True.

"I'll wait here for you."

"I want you to. It may not take but a few days." Probably not true.

"But it will likely take more, won't it?" Nothing past her.

"Yes."

"That's all right. I understand." Pause. "I'll probably go to Galveston some."

"You'll be careful when you are there." She nodded.

"I'll have a detective look in on you," I offered.

"I could go with you," she offered back.

"Yes, you could." A longer pause.

"Please be careful in New York," she finally said, deciding.

"I will send you word," I promised. She stood up, walked across the room to where I leaned against the door. Wrapped her arms around my neck.

Captain Baker and I met Frederick Rice, the brother of the old man, at the station and were on the Southern Pacific No. 36 bound for New Orleans at 7:25 p.m. The trip would take us to Grand Central Station by early morning, Thursday.

On Tuesday after we had passed New Orleans, Memphis, and were headed for Chattanooga, Baker received more telegrams from New York via Houston. The New York Detective Agency was investigating as per orders Baker had sent Monday afternoon. Rice's body was to be held at the coroner's office until Baker and Frederick Rice arrived. Cremation was still an option, but Baker wanted an autopsy first. Frederick neither agreed nor disagreed.

Over the course of the three-day trip the captain and I had an opportunity to put the first puzzle pieces on the table.

"I don't like the sound of any of this, Caleb," Baker said through a bite of breakfast muffin as we sat in the dining car early Wednesday morning. Neither of us was sleeping much, too much to ponder. I agreed with Baker's assessment so I didn't say anything. He munched some more, continued. "Coincidence. No such thing. Man dies. Lawyer's waiting at the bank vault a few hours later. Bank teller doesn't like the signature on the bank draft. I don't either." Agreed again.

"Where do you want to begin?" I offered.

"We'll head to the morgue first. Get things in order there. Let Frederick make the decisions."

"He doesn't seem to want to do that."

"Have to. It's his brother. He will when it's time." Fine by me.

"Talk to the bank folks. The detectives. Bowers and Sands." He looked at me. "We'll divide the duties. Get to it faster that way." Yes.

"You know the bank people?"

"Yep. Eric Swenson's a good man. His family owns the bank. So's Walt Wetherbee, long time clerk. Done business with them for years. Met them a coupla times when I was up."

"I'll take the detectives." Baker nodded, barely. Made sense. "What about the apartment?"

"We'll go there next. I'll meet you there. You can find it?" More of a statement than a question.

"I'll have a room full of New York detectives at my service. Probably can."

"Good." Finished breakfast. Sipped on some cooled coffee in silence. I stared out the window as Tennessee rushed by.

Thursday morning, September 27, 1900, New York City

We ended up at the apartment first after all. A brief service was held there with a local preacher mumbling a few words about a long life well-lived, or whatever. Twice a widower, home and businesses in Texas, and so on.

Eric Swenson was there. So was Wetherbee, head clerk at Swenson's bank. Charlie Jones, Mr. Rice's valet, stood off to one side and seemed to sob without making any sobbing sounds. Sort of shook through it all. Taking it hard, I supposed. Two women, elderly, dressed in black, sat in the front of the tiny congregation. They had mentioned when they first arrived that they had paid a visit the night Mr. Rice "passed." Had rung the bell several times, sent the doorman upstairs. No response. They had assumed Rice was asleep. Now it seemed otherwise.

Rice's other attorney Albert Patrick was there. Balding though still young, sideburns somewhere between beard and muttonchops, and a wide, well-groomed mustache, he stood erect at all times. His eyes sparkled. Cocky? He had just been re-tained by the Texas millionaire, he explained. Had been helping keep his business affairs in order, he said. Baker had looked at me when he heard that. Didn't know about this guy, his glance spoke loudly. I made a mental note.

The doorman stopped in and paid his respects. A neighbor or two did the same, didn't stay for the service. Out in the hall a man from the coroner's office waited patiently at the stairs. Rice's body was not there for the ceremony, but awaiting cremation. As soon as the preacher pronounced his benediction, dust and ashes, the man turned without a change of expression and headed down the stairs. Dust and ashes it would be.

Captain Baker and I accompanied the two bankers over to their institution. Met the young clerk there who had first sounded an alarm about the check to be cashed Monday morning. He said the bearer did not identify himself except as a lawyer from Mr. Rice's firm, handed him a note for $25,000 to be withdrawn on Patrick's name.

"I had never seen the man before," the clerk, John Wallace, was explaining. "The note looked authentic, but –"

"What did this man look like?" I interrupted.

"Short, medium build. Blue eyes. Blond hair?" Not balding.

"Please go on," Baker said.

"Well, it's just that Mr. Rice never did business that way. You know, sending people with notes for cash withdrawals. He just didn't do that. He either came himself, or more often got word directly to Mr. Wetherbee or Mr. Swenson. Well, they would transfer funds however he wanted. This just seemed odd, that's all." The clerk frowned as he finished. Still concerned.

"You did the right thing," Walter Wetherbee patted the man on his shoulder. He looked up at his boss, then at Baker and me, finished the story. "He excused himself from the window and came to my office immediately. Handed me the note and asked what he should do. I looked it over. Thought it was odd myself. Went out to the floor with him, introduced myself to the bearer. He said his name was Short, was from the law firm representing Mr. Rice in New York, and that Mr. Rice had sent him on this errand.

"I was looking over the note all the while – it was made out to Abert Patrick – A B E R T," he spelled the first name out. "Not Albert. I asked Mr. Short about that, showed him the note. He didn't know what to make of it. Explained he was just supposed to get the money, that was all."

"What did you do next?" Baker asked.

"I told Mr. Short we would not be able to make the transaction, that I was sorry and to please tell Mr. Rice to contact us right away. He sort of shook his head at that, like he didn't know what to do next. Took the note. Turned and walked outside."

"And that was it?" Baker raised an eyebrow.

"Oh, no sir," Wetherbee continued. "Two hours later, maybe 11:30 Monday morning, he was back at the window. Had the note endorsed again, this time with the name spelled correctly. The teller called me out there. That's when it got real curious."

"How's that, Walter?" Baker inquired.

"Well, I told Mr. Short that I was still uncomfortable about the sizable amount of money to be withdrawn, and that I would have to contact Mr. Rice personally."

"Sounds reasonable," I interjected. Eric Swenson nodded.

"But all of a sudden Short says, 'You can't do that, I'm afraid.' I asked why not, and he tells me 'Because Mr. Rice is dead.' I said 'What!' and then he tells me that Mr. Rice had been found dead during the night by his valet, and that the note had been written on Saturday but that he'd been delayed in getting down to the bank and we'd been closed Sunday, of course." The head clerk was talking rapid-fire by now.

"Slow down, Walt," Baker said. Wetherbee took a deep breath. Shut his eyes. Opened them.

"I couldn't believe what I was hearing. I went upstairs to Mr. Swenson's office to confer with him." Eric Swenson smiled as an acknowledgement. "He agreed with my assessment – that something was wrong. We went down to the floor, but by the time we got back, Mr. Short had left."

"Did he come back?" I asked.

"No sir, haven't seen him since," Walter replied.

"Do you have the note?'

"Yessir," he said. "It's in the vault in a safety deposit box."

"Leave it right there for now," Baker said.

"Yessir."

"Thanks for your help, Walter."

"Yessir."

"We're going now. Have some others we need to question." He glanced in my direction: let's go, it said.

"Yessir," Wetherbee repeated as we left the bank, nodding a goodbye to Eric Swenson.

As we walked down the sidewalk along Broadway, it occurred to me how noisy these streets were compared to Houston. Horses and carriages squeaking and clopping along the brick streets. Voices above the din. A paperboy yelling headlines incessantly. A merchant hollering about apples, another about prime cuts of beef and mutton. Doors slammed. Four boys maybe nine or ten ran in and out of the sidewalk congestion, one with a ball, another with a bat, all four shouting as they headed for the park. An inordinately tall man was bumped by one of the boys, flung curses in their direction as they laughed along. Even an automobile passed by every so often, still a marvel, an oddity.

"I'll head over to the coroner's office," Baker was saying.

"All right. I'll take the detective agency. Meet you for dinner at the hotel?"

"Sure. Good luck." I nodded. We walked a half block without speaking. At the next corner Baker turned to head on. "Don't like the Patrick story," Baker called almost over his shoulder. I nodded as we parted company. Me, neither.

The New York Detective Agency was actually subsidized by the city, at least in part. The sleuths were paid by the city of New York, although they often hired out on their own as well. The agency was housed in an old four-story graystone on Mulberry Street, twenty-five steps up from the corner at Houston Street. The Central Office of the police department also kept offices there. The head of the detective agency was George McCluskey.

Detective Sergeant Jim Vallely was there waiting for me. So was Jim Gerard, the lawyer from Bowers and Sands who first called the police in on Rice's death. Baker was looking for Gerard at this moment over at the law firm. He'd be upset when he found out the lawyer was here instead. Not my problem.

We sat in Vallely's office, amid the crumpled piles of case records and newspaper clippings and antique coffee mugs with antique coffee stains. The second floor window was shoved out into the open air, and the window sill had pigeon stains to match the coffee mugs. Vallely sat behind a desk of unimaginable jumble. Gerard sat in a cane back chair. I stood, leaning against the wall near the door.

James Vallely had a good, hard ten years on me, and it showed on calloused hands and wrinkled eyes. His handshake was firm to match his attitude. Jim Gerard, on the other hand, had been raised with a silver spoon firmly clamped between gritted teeth.

Baker had told me on the way over that the lawyer had connections all over the state, mixed comfortably with the social elite, even had a reputation as an accomplished polo player. But not soft, the captain had warned. 'He'll tell you what he thinks and there'll be no doubt about it.' Okay by me.

"We went to see Patrick Monday night," Vallely was explaining to me, so I stopped musing and started listening. He motioned toward Gerard with the 'we.' "His landlady let us in, but she didn't seem too happy about it. Her name is -" he glanced at a notebook resting on his knee - "Addie Francis. Anyway, Patrick came into the room after we'd sat down. Didn't seem at all bothered by us being there or what was going on around him."

"You mean Mr. Rice's death?" I asked for clarification. Vallely nodded.

"We talked about fifteen minutes. We asked him if he could shed any light on the old man's death. He said, yes, he believed the old man died from eating too many bananas." I probably raised an eyebrow. The detective paused a moment, then continued. "Said some old lady had told Mr. Rice that bananas were good for the elderly, and that he'd been eating them by the bunch for weeks, maybe months."

"Bananas," I said without emphasis. I would reserve that option as one near the bottom of any list I made.

"Yep. Patrick seemed to think that was it, so we changed subjects. I asked him what he knew about a check endorsed with his name on it that had been delivered to Swenson's Bank that morning. He said, yes, that was a regular activity now that he - Patrick - was Mr. Rice's attorney and - you ready for this, Lincoln?" I tried to remain calm. "Now that he was *executor* of Mr. Rice's estate." Vallely sat back in his chair, folded his hands on his lap, and stared at me as if he had just hollered checkmate.

I knew very little about all of this except what Baker had told me on the trip up from Houston. He had mentioned Mrs. Rice's contested will and the litigation that had been going on since she died. He never mentioned another will for Mr. Rice. I mulled this over for a moment, then said, "Hmm." Detective jargon.

"Absolutely," Valley sat up straight, slammed his hands palm down on the desktop for effect. "Something damn rotten about this. This guy Patrick smells like the fish market and I'll bet he's gonna be as slippery." Quaint simile. I waited. "He told us that the new will had been written up back in June and that it had been signed and sealed and registered and whatever, legal as can be. Named him as the only executor, gave him power of attorney and all that crap."

"We knew nothing about this will," Gerard spoke up for the first time since we'd come in the office. "Never notified us. I think that's odd." Agreed.

"Did he say why?" I asked.

"Yep." Vallely leaned forward, and almost in a stage whisper answered, "Said he was tired of waiting on his other lawyers down in Houston, didn't trust 'em anymore. 'Trusted me,' says Patrick." The detective sat back again. "Damnedest thing, huh, Lincoln?"

"Damnedest, Detective," I replied. But I was already thinking way ahead of where this conversation had come. If Patrick had persuaded Rice to rewrite his will back in the summer, and given himself power of attorney over all the money, was he getting impatient when the sick old man kept hanging on? Not enough bananas? Three, four months now and the old man still puttering. Was Patrick into something and owed money? Restless to get his hands on millions? Or was it just coincidence that Rice had died right after his second will had been done?

Baker had told me on the train that Mr. Rice was especially anxious the past two months to add funds to his Institute account. He wanted to see the research school started in Houston before too much longer. Said he'd told Baker and Swenson to see to it the transfers were taken care of right away.

Did Patrick know about that? Was all that money he nearly had his hands on slipping away, heading off to Houston? I made a safe wager with myself that the new will would set aside considerably less money for the university. Just a guess. I needed to get a look at that will. And have a chat with Patrick myself.

"Alibi?" I said instead. "Where was Patrick Sunday night?"

"Said he was with two women across town, giving piano lessons," Vallely remembered, didn't have to look at his notes for that one.

"And?"

"And we checked it out the next day. They'll vouch for him, all right." The detective looked disgusted.

"All night piano lessons?" I asked.

"Well, they said he was there from about seven for about three hours."

"Lots of piano playing," I mused. "Still, ten o'clock, getting back across town to murder the old man - you think he could pull that off?"

"Yep."

"Is he a suspect, then?"

"Damn right."

"Okay. Anyone else?"

"Well, the valet's another one. Lived in the apartment with the old man, watched over him, gave him his medicine."

"Bananas?"

"No, oh hell I don't know. I guess. You know what I mean." I nodded. "He was probably there the whole time."

"You talked to him? What's his name?"

"Jones. Charles Jones. From Texas originally, he says."

"And?"

"Aw, he's too soft to kill somebody," Vallely shook his head, waved a hand. "He'da puked his guts out."

"Would he have been in Rice's apartment the night of the murder?"

"Said he was, 'smatter of fact," Vallely replied. "So?"

"So," I let the word hang out there an extra beat, "if the old man was murdered, the valet either slept through a break-in and killing, or he did it himself, or he was an accomplice." I stopped. The three of us looked at each other. "I like accomplice."

"Me, too," said Gerard. Vallely nodded. Unanimous.

"I want to talk to Jones and Patrick," I said simply.

"Be my guest," the detective said. "Do you want me to set it up?"

"No. I can find them. Thanks."

"You want some company?"

"If you want." I didn't really, but it would do no harm, either.

"Tell you what," Vallely decided. "We've talked to both of them. Got damned little out of 'em, for that matter. You take a shot." I nodded okay.

"Anyone else on the short list?" I asked.

"What about the landlady?" Gerard directed his question to the detective.

"Addie Francis. Could be she knows something," he agreed. "And the piano girls."

"Anyone in Jones' life?" I was grasping at other straws. Might as well.

"I'll find out," the sergeant said. He stood up. Gerard shifted in his chair. I left the office.

17

I found Charlie Jones first, at Rice's apartment. He had been cleaning out his stuff. Had books and clothes boxed, stacked near the foyer. Not much in all. He was nervous when I introduced myself, his hands had a little shake to them. Not good, I thought. Not for him. Good for me.

"You've spoken to the police, Mr. Jones?" I began. He nodded. Sort of. Looked down mostly, not at me.

"Anything you want to add about last Sunday night?" He shook his head no. Too quickly.

"Where will you be going?" I waved my hand in the direction of the boxes. He shrugged his shoulders.

"Mebbe back to Texas," he finally spoke. Quiet voice. Timid. Shaky. This was a cold-blooded killer? Unlikely. "Got some family down there. My brothers Laf and Frank and my father, and, well -" He stopped mid-sentence. Frowned.

"What is it, Charlie?" First name. Friendly. Pals.

"I dunno." His voice quivered, went quiet. "It's just that -"

"What?" Be patient.

"Well, I've put together a good life here. Mr. Rice was good to me. I got out in the social life here in the city. Have a girl-friend. Y'know?" I nodded, knowingly I hoped. "If I go back to Texas, well, I just don't know what I'd do there. My father would take me back, I guess. I could work for my brother Frank meb-be." His voice trailed off. So had the interrogation.

Some killer, this one.

I found Albert Patrick on Saturday. He was parked in his law office in the Broadway Chambers building, 275 Broadway, 13th floor. His desk was immaculate, no piles of paper, nothing out of place. His whole office looked like no one ever worked there. But Patrick was working. When I walked in he had his head down over a sheaf of papers, scribbling like mad, turning sheets over, underlining, poking at the notes with the tip of his pencil. So engrossed I had to speak first to get noticed. He looked up, squinted as if changing the gears of the machine in his head, pro-cessing. We had seen each other at the funeral service but had not formally met. He seemed to be reaching deep for my name. Finally gave up - all of this in an instant - stood with a broad smile on his face, walked around his desk and right up to me, hand thrust out far ahead of him.

"Nice to see you again," he began.

"Caleb Lincoln, Pinkerton's," I finished his thought for him.

"Of course, Mr. Lincoln." Like I had insulted him. Still the large grin. "Please sit down. What brings you to my domain?" I sat. Domain.

"Working on the investigation," I said.

"Investigation?" His eyebrows raised. "Of what, pray tell?"

"Mr. Rice's death."

"Mr. Rice died of old age, Mr. Lincoln. He had been quite ill, you know."

"So I understand. In his eighties, too." Patrick nodded, too eagerly. "Still, Captain Baker thinks we should take a look about while we're here."

"And what would you be looking for?" Still the smile, now with an edge to it.

"Not sure," I said. Partly true. "There seem to be some discrepancies."

"Oh? In what way, if you don't mind my asking?"

"Don't mind a bit. Some have suggested that Mr. Rice was in fairly good health."

"Not so," Patrick said too quickly.

"Uh huh. A bit concerned with the check that was brought to the bank Monday morning."

"That was from my office. Standard procedure. Bad timing."

"Seemed odd," I pushed on the subject. "Large amount. No word initially that Mr. Rice had passed away a few hours earlier." I emphasized hours.

"David, uh, Mr. Short, had no way of knowing that Rice was dead. Charlie knew. He contacted me later that night. And the doorman. That's all."

"The new will -"

"Now, Mr. Lincoln," Patrick interrupted me. The smile had hardened. "Captain Baker and the police detectives and I have been over this in great detail. There is nothing out of the ordinary about any of this." He took a deep breath, as if to begin a lesson that I obviously needed. Oh boy. "When a wealthy man passes on," Patrick's voice was dripping with condescension, "it often complicates a situation already complex in nature. Estates, wills, great amounts of monies changing hands, business being taken care of in the midst of it all. You understand?" I nodded. How sweet to ask. He went on. "I assure you there is nothing out of the ordinary here. Except for Mr. Rice's untimely passing."

"I am reassured," I said. Patrick blinked. His smile wavered, returned in full.

"I suspect that Captain Baker is concerned with his relationship to the Rice estate. That is, he may have stood to gain a great deal upon Mr. Rice's death."

"No, I don't think that has anything to do with the captain's concerns," I replied firmly.

"Oh? And what, pray tell, would his concern be?"

I wanted to shove the pray tell back down his throat. I controlled myself.

"The Institute," I said instead. And politely.

"Ah, yes. The Institute." Patrick's smile got bigger, brighter. Faker. "Mr. Rice had a soft spot for that project, to be sure. He and I had many conversations regarding the Houston school." Somehow I doubted that. "If you will allow me, I would want you to know that the amount of monies set aside for the Institute remain unchanged in the new will. That was an absolute priority for Mr. Rice."

"What a relief."

"And if we can find a way to invest those funds in order for the amount to even increase over these next months until the will is probated, that would suit me just fine. A testimonial to Mr. Rice's memory, if you will." He reached his hands over his head as if displaying a sign. "The Rice Institute, perhaps."

"Perhaps. Anything else you might want to add that you had failed to tell the detectives, Mr. Patrick?"

"Not a syllable, Mr. Lincoln." The smile was cracking like a granite statue.

"You've been most helpful." I stood. He did not offer his hand. I started out.

"Oh, Mr. Lincoln," Patrick's voice sounded almost sweet. "One more thing." I turned back to him. "Do you think this investigation will be finalized soon?"

"Don't know," I said.

"Maybe it should," he suggested. "For everyone's sake."

I returned to the detective agency. Vallely was gone until Monday. Two other detectives were there, and they had messages for me when I arrived.

The police had followed up on my request already regarding friends or acquaintances of Charlie Jones there in New York. He seemed to be the softest point of this investigation, the best place to work. George Gordon Battle was a friend of his, a pretty high-powered attorney there in the city, I was told. An Alexander Stanbery was mentioned in the report. He had worked with Mr. Rice on the estate of Rice's second wife, done some traveling for him to Wisconsin, and kept an active correspondence through Jones.

There was an estate in New Jersey where Rice had often gone to work. Jones had always accompanied him there. It seemed like a good lead.

But the girlfriend was the best part. Three detectives had interviewed people in the building where Rice lived along with neighborhood stores and businesses on Madison Avenue. Charlie Jones was quite the ladies' man by all accounts. Did he have a steady girl, they asked. Absolutely, the answer came. Then the fun part: not one steady girl, but three. Maude Mortimer, one had told the police. No, her name was Mabel Whitney, insisted another. And a beauty named Nellie Creed was the third.

Busy young man. While feeding bananas, or something, to an old man. And assisting in his murder.

On Saturday evening just past sundown, I stood outside a red brick two-story off Broadway and knocked at Nellie Creed's door. The woman who answered my knock was the kind who took your breath away. Auburn hair that drifted more or less under control across rosied cheeks and supple shoulders. Not tall by any means but with a charm that towered over everyone around her. Deep black eyes, charismatic.

Nellie met me at the door in an evening lingerie, black as her eyes, cut - well, everywhere to show nearly everything. Bright red lipstick set off the black and the ivory flesh tones. I had the notion she met everyone at her door in the same engaging, black widow manner. Please come in, let me eat you alive.

"Please come in," she said in a dripping honey voice, "won't you?" She didn't exactly smile, but the pouty expression on her lips magnetized. I stepped inside, thinking I had already made a mistake.

"My name is Caleb Lincoln," I introduced myself. She put her hand on my wrist, letting her long, red-nailed fingers slip down across the back of my hand. Something deep inside of me shuddered. Oh my.

"I'm Nellie Creed," she said but didn't have to, "and I am pleased to make your acquaintance." Said the spider to the fly. "Please sit with me in the parlor." She turned deftly on a heel and started across the hall, disappearing for a moment through a passageway. I followed her into a dimly-lit parlor with too much furniture. A huge armoire covered one wall, with trees and plants and floral arrangements scattered everywhere. There were more dressers and small tables. An oriental carpet adorned the center of the room. On it sat a burgundy velvet loveseat.

Nellie Creed took me by the hand and led me into her lair, sitting us on the cozy loveseat, her hip snug against mine. "Now, Mr. Lincoln," she said, almost whispering in my ear, "what in the world can I do for you?" Like she meant it.

"I'm investigating the death of Mr. William Marsh Rice," I said. I was proud that the words came easily, that I was breathing normally.

"Mr. Rice?" she said, not sure of the name at first.

"On Madison Avenue," I explained.

"Oh, yes, of course," she answered quickly. "Charlie's employer."

"Yes, that's right."

"Charlie told me the poor old man had finally passed on." Deep pout.

"Last Sunday night," I said unnecessarily.

"Yes. And you think my Charlie killed him?"

She was several remarks ahead of me, and I needed to catch up.

"No, ma'am," I tried to slow her down. "I'm just trying to learn what I can about Mr. Rice's death."

"But you think he was murdered, don't you? That's why you're investigating." She said the last word by syllables, and patted my arm with her hand for each one.

"We believe there may be some questions that need better answers than have come along so far."

"For instance?"

"For instance, did Mr. Jones ever talk to you about Mr. Rice's health?"

"Are you related to the late president of our United States?"

"Excuse me?"

"Are you related to -" I raised a hand.

"No, I'm not. I was born on the day he died. April 15, 1865. My mother gave me his name."

"Hmm," Nellie Creed purred. "Not hers?"

This conversation had now gone into the ditch.

"Miss Creed," I started again, "do you have any information about Mr. Rice that you might want to share with me?"

"I don't think Charlie could have ever done anything as awful as kill someone. Do you?" No, I didn't. His girlfriend, yes. Charlie, not by himself.

"We don't know that there has been a murder at all, Miss Creed."

"Nellie, please."

"Miss Creed," I decided to remain strong.

"Mr. Lincoln," her hand running from her lap over onto mine. Strong was a relative term. "Mr. Lincoln, I really don't know that much about what Charlie did over at Mr. Rice's home." Her voice raised about an octave.

"Did you ever go over to Mr. Rice's apartment to see Charlie?" Her hand stayed on my thigh. I was considering moving it off over the next decade or so.

"Yes," she said slowly. "Charlie invited me over a couple of times." She looked up to the ceiling and sort of chuckled to herself. "Mr. Rice slept very hard at night. Wouldn't hear a thing going on around him." She looked right into my eyes. The magnetic charge was palpable.

"Miss Creed, if you can think of anything that might be helpful to this investigation, I hope you will contact me. I expect to be in the city for a couple of weeks at least."

She squeezed my upper leg. "You could stay for a bit," she whispered.

"What a treat." I'd had enough.

"Bastard," she said without changing the tone of her voice.

"To be sure," I said. I let myself out.

"My Son," she was saying as I lay dozing with my head in her lap, *"you were born on an important day, the day our president died. I was staying in a hotel in Washington, D.C., a rundown place next to the theatre. I had been working at Ford's, sewing costumes and selling tickets and whatever else they needed.*

"Friday night the play was going on and the crowd was laughing. I was sitting in the very back row, under the central balcony. The president and Mrs. Lincoln were there, up in a private box. They had arrived after the curtain had gone up. The play had stopped and the audience stood and applauded the man who had brought the awful war to an end.

There was a commotion. People stood up from their seats and stared. The play halted. A man leaped down onto the stage, rolled to his side. He stood up - I think he broke his ankle when he jumped - and shouted something at the audience. Then he ran out the back of the stage. Somebody

*yelled that the president had been shot. Everyone screamed and ran in
every direction.*

*"Except me. I had just gone into labor. The pain held me down and
I couldn't move. Nearly everyone had left the theatre, and some soldiers
had carried Mr. Lincoln out. A nice gentleman saw me and helped me
back to my room in the hotel. He called for a neighbor I knew there who
was a midwife.*

*"It lasted the night through. About seven the next morning someone
rang a bell out in the street. It sounded so very sad. I knew what it meant.*

*"And you were born a few minutes later. I had always known I would
name a son Caleb, after my brother who had died in Mexico in the other
war. But I didn't know your father and wanted you to have a strong, good
name to live by. Caleb Lincoln. My dear, dear son."*

And I fell asleep.

Sunday, September 30, 1900. One week after Rice's death, four
weeks and a day since the hurricane.

I thought about Abbie. A lot. We had swapped telegrams. She
was fine. Working hard in Galveston still. I told her what I could
about the investigation. Not much to tell so far, I admitted.
Captain Baker and I had walked miles of New York City side-
walks, interviewed dozens, talked to the police, to suspects and
their acquaintances. Not much but suspicions.

The coroner's report would give us some clues. Anything on the new will might lead us somewhere. Perhaps someone would break down and confess. Maybe the sun wouldn't come up at dawn.

Baker went on interviewing, scouring files and reports and records with Gerard at Bowers & Sands. Albert Patrick worked on as if nothing had happened. Charlie Jones moved in with a friend across town.

I went to New Jersey.

William Marsh Rice's second wife had wanted nothing to do with Texas. A midwesterner, she disliked New York except for the social climb it meant for her, sweeping from ball to banquet with Astors and the like. But the city got to both of them sometimes, according to friends and business associates. He had purchased an estate out in Somerset County, New Jersey, a getaway place to appease her and, at least occasionally, provide a respite for him. They had had the place for years, well-kept by a staff during their prolonged absences, well cared for when they resided there.

I had no idea what I might find in New Jersey. Just another trail to follow. What I found was Feenie Trust and trouble.

Josephine Trust was a neighbor whose own palatial estate stood within sight of the Rice's front porch on the next rise. Their closest neighbor, she had dined with them on many occasions over the years. She was in her sixties, handsome and alive and filled with the energy that comes with good country living.

"Mrs. Rice loved it here," she told me. "She hated the city, hated Texas, hated traveling. She longed to be here, to stay here. But Mr. Rice would grow restless after just a few days. He'd take off for the city, days at a time, then come back for her. She was uncomfortable out here alone, so we'd visit a great deal then. He'd talk her into going to New York with him, or take a trip to Albany or Boston or maybe Kansas City. She'd cry every time they rode away."

"Did Mr. Rice take care of business out here?"

"Oh, some I suppose. He had an office upstairs. There," she pointed from her porch, "that corner window on the upper left."

"Did business associates come out here often?"

"No, not often. Some. A carriage would come out from the station with two or three men in it. Sometimes they'd have a box of papers and such."

"Do you remember the last time Mr. Rice came out here, Mrs. Trust?"

"Feenie. Everybody calls me Feenie."

"Feenie."

"Well, he was out early last summer. Mid June, perhaps. Stayed about a week."

"Was he alone?"

"Yes. Well, most of it. Two men rode out for a day, didn't stay overnight."

"Did you see them? Could you describe them?"

"They were both tall, over six feet. Dark hair, both of them. Clean shaven." Bless nosy neighbors.

"Had you ever seen them before, Feenie?"

"No."

"Thank you, Feenie. If you think of anything else, please let me know. You can contact Bowers & Sands in the city." I kissed her on the cheek.

"Why, Mr. Lincoln," she said, and laughed a hearty laugh as I rode away.

It hadn't been Patrick or Jones. That left the rest of the men in the Western Hemisphere. I was reasonably sure by this time that Patrick may not have ever met Rice. The will had been worked over in the background. Jones had been the go-between, the messenger, maybe unwittingly, giving information that Patrick needed to work his scheme. Charlie, the perfect foil. Others were in it, I was pretty sure of that as well, although Patrick had to be the ringleader. He had the stuff. Maybe his partners, Meyers or Potts or Short were their names according to the listing on the office door.

The shot rang out from behind me and to the right, and I heard it like some background noise in a play. Not sure of what it was or what it had to do with me, until the bullet whizzed past my ear, clipping a tree limb just beyond where I rode along. I slid over in the saddle until the horse was between me and the source of that shot, urging the mount a little faster. A mott of trees engulfed me for the moment.

I pulled the horse up quickly, dismounted as he slowed, and gave him a slap on the rump with my hand. He took off down the road for town. I rolled into the hedges and pulled my pistol out in the same motion. I nestled up against a maple tree's trunk and waited.

Only a minute passed before they rode up. Two men on horseback, bowler hats and black dusters, rifles at the ready. They slowed as they entered the little haven of trees that enveloped the road for about fifty yards. Eyes darting everywhere, into the shadows where I hid. They walked their mounts twenty paces along and had passed me by ten feet when I stepped out behind them.

"You gentlemen lost?" I asked casually, my gun directed at a point between them. They halted in one motion. Didn't look back.

"We're looking for poachers," one of them called without turning around.

"Haven't seen any," I called back.

"Then we'll be moving on." The same voice.

"Maybe not," I answered. "Maybe you can tell me first who's been shooting at my right ear."

"Wouldn't know about that, mister," Same Voice said.

"Wonder if I could check your rifle," I was pretty sure I knew the answer.

"Don't think that would be a possibility."

"Thought I'd ask first. Throw your rifles down, carefully," I instructed, "then get down." I aimed my gun at Same Voice.

"Can't do that, mister. Gotta be going on to town now."

"That would be a big mistake," I replied.

"You armed, mister?"

"What would be your guess?"

"You think you can hit both of us before we get you?" Well, yes.

"I can sure get you first. Then we'll see what's left."

There was a long pause. Maybe ten counts. The quiet one made the first move, striking his heels into his horse's side, bending forward against its neck as it took off into the ditch to my right. I swung my pistol and shot him just above the waist, the bullet probably climbing up through his spine and headed for his neck. He catapulted over his horse's head with the impact and somersaulted into a heap in the ditch he'd been headed for.

The talkative one had swung around in his saddle, rifle leading, hoping to beat my response by an instant. He didn't. My second bullet bored a hole right between his shocked eyes, tearing the back of his head out like a smashed pumpkin. He sat up straight for a moment, already dead, then fell over onto the road.

I put the two bodies over the back of the larger of the two horses, mounted the other one, and rode into town.

18

No one recognized either of the bodies I brought in. The local sheriff had a long chat with me, something about not coming back to New Jersey in this lifetime, scattering bodies around his precinct, and so on. He was not inclined to arrest me. I guess he believed my story. With no eyewitnesses, I might have been in a certain amount of trouble had he not. The Pinkerton badge helped. So did Vallely's name which he recognized.

I was back in the city by nightfall. But I had a whole lot more questions than answers now. Like why was I still a target? And was the latest try related to what had happened in Houston? Surely it was related to the Rice investigation, but how? Who would want me dead? What did I know that was so damn valuable? The connections between Houston and

Galveston and New York City had to be there: I just couldn't figure it out. Yet.

Well, if I could stay alive long enough.

Monday, October 1, 1900   New York City

Detective Sergeant James Vallely was preparing arrest warrants for Albert Patrick and Charles Jones. The warrants mentioned premeditated murder and falsifying documents related to the estate of the late William Marsh Rice. He was bluffing. I knew it. Patrick would, too. It was Jones he thought he could break.

"I think you need to hold off on the arrests," I was saying as we sat in an outer office at the police precinct station house. "Patrick will see through it. If he warns Jones, we'll lose him, too." Vallely knew I was right. He hated that.

"Your suggestion?" he asked with a large dose of frustration in his tone.

"We wait for the coroner's report. If he finds something we can connect to Patrick or Jones, that's the premeditation you need."

"And if he doesn't find anything?"

"Then we bluff. Won't work though," I added. Vallely harumphed.

"Screw it. I think we go with it anyway. Jones'll break."

"Not if Patrick gets to him."

"We can keep them apart until then."

"Really? How? Tell them they've been bad boys and can't see each other?"

"Put 'em under house arrest, maybe. Keep a detective on 'em. Hell, I don't know." He was exasperated. I didn't blame him.

"We could shoot one of them and put him in the hospital," I suggested.

"Wha-? Oh hell, Lincoln. You're no help with this situation."

"It's what I do best."

"Whatever. Get Baker over here. Let's see what he's got."

Captain Baker had very little more than the rest of us. He agreed with me that there had to be a connection between the Galveston murder and Rice, but with little proof of that we were still empty handed. The coroner thought it would be three or four more weeks until his report was finished – that was too long to expect Patrick couldn't get to the weaker Jones. Baker suggested we go with the will.

"If Patrick and whoever else wrote up that will without Mr. Rice's knowledge, whose signature is on it?" he asked. If it was Rice, he had to have been fooled into it – not a likely possibility.

More likely: someone forged the old man's signature. My guess: Patrick. Baker agreed.

"We push on the signature, then," Baker said and everyone in the office nodded or murmured agreement. "We need copies of Rice's signature from any records we can get. Bowers & Sands will have some. I can get some delivered from my Houston office by Wednesday night. Swenson's Bank will have some, too."

We went to work. By Thursday morning, October 4, we had a stack of papers in front of us, checks and receipts and business orders, everyone with the scribbled name of William M. Rice somewhere on it. Between Eric Swenson, Jim Gerard, and the captain, we believed every one of these to be authentic.

Then we put them up against one another. Found the peculiar marks, the curves and breaks and anything that matched 99 times out of a hundred. Next we put the will to the test, pulled from the safety deposit box with Patrick's oddly eager permission. Almost too eager, I thought. He's either got ice water in his veins or he was telling the truth about the new will. I wanted the chance to open one of those veins, watch the ice cubes fall out.

The signatures didn't match. Very, very close. But the will was a phony. We had him. Late in the afternoon on Thursday, October 4, the New York police rounded up Albert Patrick and

Charlie Jones, served them with warrants accusing them of forgery and conspiracy. Neither resisted. Charlie Jones broke into a cold sweat and nearly sobbed as he was brought in. Patrick was all smiles.

I wanted him very badly.

For the moment, though, I decided to return to Houston.

I took the first train out of New York City's Grand Central Station on Saturday morning, October 6, headed for Texas. The eventual arrival late Monday night gave me plenty of time to ponder the mysterious case of William Marsh Rice's death. On the one hand, and without any more evidence than we already had mustered, it could have been of natural causes. In addition, the new will from June might still be validated in a court of law, although unlikely. If Patrick had any connections with crooked New York judges – I wouldn't be surprised – he could still get off Scot free and with nearly half a million bucks to see him into his golden years.

Second possibility: death by natural causes but a conspiracy and a forged will. It's what we had at the moment, and it would do. But Patrick would be out of the Tombs in a year, Charlie probably less as nothing but a weak accomplice. Maybe get Patrick's firm behind bars for awhile, get them closed down maybe. Maybe not.

Best scenario for Baker and me: conspiracy, forgery, murder. First degree. Twenty to life. Odds: slim. Hope: springing eternal.

The key was still Galveston. And I didn't know what it was. Someone did. It's why I'd been attacked in two states. A murder in the castle. A prescription in a dead man's hand. A death in New York City. A bad will. And a red-haired man who wanted me as badly as I wanted him. At least now I was pretty sure who was behind the effort to take me out of the investigation. And Patrick had the money and the man power to make it happen.

The train hadn't made it much past Philadelphia when I realized this case was still far from over.

I had left the dining car late Saturday evening and was headed three cars distance to the Pullman, upper suite 6B. The aisle was narrow and twice I had to lean hard against the wall as other passengers met me. A couple was looking for their sleeping quarters, and she kept mumbling about his getting them lost. A few steps later I encountered two men in suits walking deliberately my way. I pushed to my right to let them by, but was sure to catch the eye of the first. He was squinting – in the dark aisle? – and his brow furrowed as I got a close-up look.

I was ready as he passed and the two had me sandwiched between them. The one behind stopped and spread his feet apart in a stance that meant business. The frowning one turned too suddenly and gave himself away in that split second. I hit him on the jaw while he was still slightly off balance from the turn, and followed the punch with the rest of my body right through him. I shoved him easily onto the floor of the car as he reeled from the calculated blow, and stepped squarely on his chest as I dove forward. He grunted and lay where he'd slammed to the ground.

I didn't bother to look back. The other guy was bound to be after me. I hit the doors where the two cars joined, feeling the brisk night air as I moved through and into the next Pullman. I heard the doors slam behind me as I pushed on, feet scrambling along the thin, worn carpet. At the end of the second car, as I shoved through the door, I glanced over my shoulder. My pursuer was still five strides behind me, and I could see what looked like a billy club in one hand. Great. I had a gun on my hip, but shooting on a train was like a gallery at a carnival: bullets ricocheting and innocents toppling.

I kept moving. As I reached the dining car I made a decision. With only two cars left I could not run forever. Hadn't planned to anyhow. I slowed my pace as I entered the now-emptied diner, allowing Billy Club to inch closer. A lonely waiter in white jacket and gloves looked up from a far table, alarmed when he saw the chase coming his way. The fourth table on my right was still set, maybe for a late midnight supper. In one motion I grabbed an ivory dinner plate, stopped on my right foot, and shifted my weight hard to my left leg as I swung. The startled suit had no chance to dodge. He lifted his weapon to shoulder height. I hit him across the face with the plate. It shattered with an explosive sound into a thousand pieces that flew all across the car. He came upright as he halted. I countered with a left hook that caught him flush on his jaw. He spun around and fell face first to the floor, his club rolling under a dining table.

I pressed my knee into the small of his back and with my right hand I clutched at the back of his neck. I slammed his head into the floor twice and he stopped writhing. I knew he wasn't dead. I had several questions I needed answering. To make sure he was unconscious, though, I held him in that position for a few more seconds.

That was my only mistake. With my head down, concentrating on this guy, I never saw the other one. Whatever he hit me with, it drove me to the floor in a heap on top of the guy I'd just taken down. A white light seared through my brain like a strike of lightning, but I didn't black out. Instead, I pulled up on my elbows and looked up. The toe of his shoe caught me under my chin and I flew in a clumsy back somersault onto my shoulder blades.

I rolled to my left side as he came at me, reaching instinctively for the pistol at my side. He saw what I was doing at the same instant. Grabbed a tablecloth in reach and threw it at my face. It draped over me as I worked to get some balance and draw my gun. I sat hard on my butt, revolver now in hand, and grabbed at the cloth with my left. Waiting for the next blow at each second that passed, I winced in anticipation. But no blow came.

I finally pulled the cloth to one side, pistol now in both hands, pointed. The door at the end of the dining car swung shut even as I focused in the kerosene lamplight. I could barely make out the silhouette of my attacker. He was facing me, hunched over, dragging his buddy out of the car with him. Then in the next instant he was gone.

I pulled myself to my feet, off balance and in a narrow place and with gun in one hand and damn my chin hurt. It seemed to take half the night just to stand up. I looked over my shoulder. The waiter stood stock still where'd he been when I first came in the car, still bent over a table, his eyes wide and white and frightened. Not a muscle moved.

"See you at breakfast," I called out as I headed for the door.

"Yassuh," came the tentative reply.

By the time I reached the next car, they were gone. They could've been in any dark hiding place. They could've leaped off the train, or walked calmly away at any of the stops that came and went as we headed south. I never saw them again.

Three states, then. What was it I knew that was so damned important I had to be silenced?

19

By the time the train ground to a halt at the Houston station, the only thing that hurt worse than my jaw was a sinking sensation somewhere deep inside that Abbie was in trouble. I rushed to the hotel and tore up the stairs to our room.

The place was ripped to shreds. Furniture keeled over, drawers pulled open and dumped, piles of clothes strewn about. One set of window curtains lay in a heap below the sill. Two paintings were torn down the middle but raggedly hung onto their frames. A small dresser mirror displayed an unwieldy crack across its face as it lay on its side. A hairbrush leaned against the door frame.

Abbie was gone.

I made absolutely sure before I left, checked the two closets and the private bathroom. Clothes and towels spread in all directions, no sign of anything gone that I noticed. Except her.

I ran double-steps down to the foyer, hollered for the manager who came running, his eyes wide. No, sir, no one had seen or heard anything. No, we didn't know there had been a break-in. Yes, we'd call the police immediately. The young woman? No, she hadn't been seen since the night before, returning from dinner and escorted to her door by a deputy.

I slammed my fist hard on the registry desk, muttered something unintelligible even to me, and stalked out into the mid-morning air. It was cool and humid, typically Houston. A breeze blew fitfully from the south. People were walking or riding by as if nothing had happened. What did they know?

I took several steps up the street, stopped. Turned on my heel and walked back past the hotel entrance and half a block that direction. Stopped. What the hell was I doing? Expecting Abbie to appear suddenly from around the corner, either safe or in the clutches of some adversary? Waiting for someone to shout at me that they had just seen her moments earlier?

It was probable that she had been taken during the night, well after midnight when the late shift slept through its responsibilities. No desk clerk, no doorman, no maids in the hallways. No witnesses. No clues.

I walked back inside the hotel and waited for the police to arrive. They were there in ten minutes, two detectives neither of whom I recognized. We walked up to the room, where the three of us surveyed the damage. One of the detectives had a notepad and he wrote constantly as we shuffled about inside the apartment. They did not speak except to each other, quietly.

After five minutes or so we walked out into the hallway. The taller of the two officers, the one without the pad, spoke up first.

"Mr. Lincoln, is it?" I nodded. "Mr. Lincoln, when did you last see, uh-"

"Abigail Scarborough," I filled in the blank and then answered. "Nearly two weeks ago. I've been on business in New York City with Captain James Baker."

"The Rice case?" the detective asked suddenly as the name registered.

"Yes. I received a telegram from Abbie, Miss Scarborough," I corrected myself, "three days ago, just before I left on the train."

"Nothing since?"

"No."

"So something," he motioned with a hand toward the open door of the apartment, "could have occurred anytime in the last seventy-two hours?"

"Yes." And a trail growing colder, I thought to myself in frustration.

"Do you have any idea who might have done this?" I shook my head. "Do you know why Miss Scarborough might have been a target of kidnappers?"

"No," I suppose that was a lie, but I didn't know what connection there could be to any of this and her. Except me.

"Any old boyfriends?"

"No," I growled.

"Ex husband?"

"No."

"Someone looking for you?"

I started down the hall for the stairs. The detective placed his hand on my arm as I passed. I stopped, looked down at his hand. And into his eyes. He withdrew his hand.

"Make sure we can find you, Mr. Lincoln," he called out as I walked away. "Don't leave Houston." I turned the corner.

The world had turned completely black and cold. Abbie could feel the rope around her wrists, tight but not painfully so. The hood over her head kept her in a personal darkness. She lay on her left side on the ground, prickly pebbles making an uncomfortable bedding beneath her. She was pretty sure she was inside a building of some kind because of the stifling air she tried to breathe through the hood. It was very quiet, no sounds of birds or crickets or coyotes or her captors.

She had lost track of time, but a growling stomach and dry throat told her it had been more than twenty-four hours since she had been kidnapped from her apartment. They had come in the night, picking the lock on the door and forcing their way into the bedroom where she slept. She had put up a fight, drawing blood on arms and faces while they clamped rough hands over her mouth to keep her from screaming an alarm. The hood and ropes had gone on quickly and she was dragged to the door still in her negligee. One of them had pushed his hand up her thigh as she lay there. Another had grunted some command and the hand withdrew. She felt vulnerable and helpless, which made her furious.

She had listened as they methodically tore the apartment to shreds. Tables and chairs toppled, clothes ripped from closets and drawers. They looked for something - she had no idea what it might be - and finally gave up, she supposed. One of them hoisted her onto his shoulder, her head lolling at his back as they marched down the stairs and outside. She wondered why no one saw them, even though it was well past midnight. A night clerk? No one to stop them?

Laid into the bed of a hay wagon - she could feel and smell the straw - Abbie lay still as the cart rolled down the brick street, bumping and cajoling her. Then onto what may have been a dirt road. She wriggled as the trip went on into the early hours before dawn, trying to loosen the ropes and get free from whoever they were. Failing that and exhausted, she lay quietly for the last leg of the mysterious journey. She imagined Cale appearing out of the shadows and rescuing her. She closed her eyes tightly several times, willing the dream to come true, even though she knew her love was hundreds of miles away.

As dark as the hood was she could tell when the sun arose, for the black of her world turned shades of gray with first light. The wagon stopped suddenly, skidding her across its bed and against one side. Lifted *again, she found some energy deep within to struggle once more. Her captor nearly dropped her as he carried her twenty steps or so, wrestling his burden back over his shoulder.*

Then she was unceremoniously dumped into another depository. This one swayed and dipped with her weight. A boat! She heard the oars, felt the weight of others clambering into the vessel with her, pushed off into the river or lake or ocean or wherever she was. She guessed the voyage to be less than thirty minutes. A bump, more movement, voices now at normal volume, oars put up, back roughly onto a shoulder. Abbie made a mental note to identify this one and return the jostling favor some day.

Deposited in a shed or cabin now, many hours had passed. She had slept fitfully, awakened at every tiny noise, drifted and dreamed and hoped and prayed. The darkness did not frighten her, but the loneliness and helplessness did have its effect. She needed Cale to come. Meanwhile she would continue her attempt to escape.

I had spoken to a dozen people before I hit pay dirt. It had become obvious that the kidnapping had taken place during the night, but I kept knocking on doors and stopping folks in front of the hotel anyway. Had they seen anything? Any strange noises? Any suspicious characters? All had confessed to being of no help until I tried a second time with the night clerk.

"Well, sir," the young man with a pockmarked face confessed, "I wasn't at the desk the *whole* time night before last."

"You told me before you never left your post," I said irritably.

"I know. I was afraid the manager would fire me," he said, his voice shaky.

"We'll just keep this our little secret," I said in a stage whisper, wanting to strangle the information out of him.

"Okay. Thanks." He paused. I frowned hard. He gulped. "Oh, yeah. Well, it was just after two o'clock, I guess, night before last. A man came in, asked me if the telegraph was working. I said yes sir we keep it twenty-four hours for our patrons. He said fine he wanted to send a telegram to San Francisco right away. He handed me a silver dollar piece. I went across the lobby, unlocked the telly office. He followed me in, closed the door behind us. I thought that was kinda weird." He stopped. I frowned again, showing great restraint. He continued, "So anyhow he had trouble trying to remember the address. Then he couldn't decide how he wanted the message to go." Each sentence he ended as if it was a question. "He kept starting over. I'd write it down. He'd say no that's not right, so I'd scratch it out. He'd think awhile, then we'd do it again."

"How long were you in the office?" I offered. He furrowed his brow.

"Mebbe ten, twelve minutes, I'd say." Long enough, I thought.

"Did you see or hear anything out in the lobby during that time?"

"Uh, no. He had me pretty busy working on the telly. I was bent over at the desk, see -" I nodded. Get on with it. "And he was kinda between me and the door, y'know." Uh huh. "Anyhow, he finally said never mind he'd have to think about it and he'd come back in the morning when he had it figgered out." The desk clerk stopped, thought it over a few seconds. "Guess what?"

"He never came back," I took a wild guess.

"You're right, mister," the boy was awed. "Geez."

"Thanks," I said. Awe inspiring. "Describe the man." He did, but it didn't help. "Did you see him leave?"

"Yessir. Walked him to the front door. He got into a wagon with two other men, rode off thataway." He pointed up the street. "One of the fellas was in the back of the wagon." So was Abbie, I thought to myself as I left the hotel.

Abbie managed to nudge her way across the dirt floor of the shed by pulling her knees up high and then pushing off like she was swimming. It seemed to take forever, and she couldn't see where she was headed, and didn't know that it would make any difference anyway. But dammit she had to do something, not just lie there and wait for. . .whatever. Besides, it made the time go by a little faster. Doing something.

In what was probably a few minutes but seemed like hours, she took one last slide and bumped her head, hard, into the wall. She bit her lip to keep from hollering out in pain. Her head throbbed. But she had gotten somewhere and it made her feel like she had accomplished something.

Abbie pushed with her heels until she had swung herself around face front to the wall. Her hands tied in front of her allowed her to at least feel the dirt and now the crevice where the shed almost met the ground. For a brief moment she considered digging her way under the shed wall and to freedom, but the prospect was ridiculously impossible. *Fingernails scratching away for months,* she thought to herself. *Like some prisoner digging away forever.*

As she moved her hands in small circles along the edge of the wall, a sharp stabbing pain suddenly shot through one finger. She bent the fingers into a fist in response, clinched tight to stop the pain. A moment passed. She touched the tip of the wounded finger with her thumb, felt the blood, squeezed hard against the puncture for a full minute. She couldn't see but imagined the bleeding had stopped. Gingerly let her fingers crawl back to the same spot until she touched the object that had surprised her. It felt like a small piece of glass. Perhaps a window somewhere above her was shattered, shards like this one laying about on the floor.

Abbie gripped the piece of glass between thumb and forefinger and turned it carefully in her grasp until the sharp edge lay against the rope that bound her wrists. The rope had little give and her hands were small and her fingers tired like the rest of her. But she began to saw against the rope with the makeshift knife. It seemed to make little headway, and she stopped often, wearied and strained. She could not tell if it was working, but she kept at it.

A creaking noise, a latch thrown, and a door across from where the girl lay pushed open. Abbie lay motionless, let the glass drop silently to the ground. The footsteps were quiet on the soil, but she heard, or felt, them as they approached. She felt more vulnerable than ever, her negligee now tattered and dirty and still all she had on, drawn up onto her hips from her crawl across the shed floor.

The footsteps stopped very near her. She could hear the man breathing directly above her. His breathing was heavy, and not from toil she guessed. She could feel his eyes staring down on her, and she could do nothing. The stranger bent down over her, and she could smell his breath through the fabric of the hood draped over her. A strong hand grabbed her left shoulder and pushed it down to the ground. Abbie's hips turned with the same motion until she lay flat on her back. She tried to pull her legs together but the man's feet were firmly planted in-between. She could feel his awful stare above her like a burning match edging along only inches away from her body.

The stranger stood up straight, and with a noise somewhere between a grunt and a chuckle, unclasped the belt of his pants.

In one fluid move Abbie bent her knees, pulled her legs up to her torso and together at the heels, and drove her long legs forward and upward with all the strength she could muster. Her aim, though blind, was right on the mark. Both heels slammed into the man's groin, sending him *reeling backward and off balance. His pants slid down to his knees even as he threw his arms back to catch himself. With no way to regain his balance in that instant, he kicked out with one leg that was caught in his pants, further throwing him akilter. Abbie heard the breath spew out of him with a loud harumph as he hit the ground shoulder blades first.*

An extended moan echoed across the shed from where he lay, followed after about thirty seconds with a flurry of curses that bounced off the walls like ricocheting bullets. Abbie pulled her knees up and together, and waited for the blow sure to come. She had at least made it unpleasant for him before he would have his way with her.

Running footsteps. Another stranger now at the door. Abbie closed her eyes tightly. A grumble from the man she had struck down. Then a bellowing laugh from the other at what must have been a curious, pathetic sight. She could hear shuffling and grunts, and more profanity, another big, deep laugh.

And then the footsteps, two pair, marched away. The shed door closed. A latch clicked. And it was silent again.

I lost the trail. It had been a long shot, anyway, with a wagon's midnight ride through the streets of the city. No possibility of tracking the kidnappers, even though I walked a hundred blocks that day. I did find a night shift constable who had spotted just such a wagon - three occupants, he recalled vaguely. He had been walking his beat ten blocks east of downtown and the hotel where

Abbie had been taken. Saw the wagon ambling along sometime around three, he thought. Nothing out of the ordinary except the hour. One of the men had waved in his direction and he back. Then the wagon had disappeared in the darkness.

I widened my range and to the east, but by dusk I had nothing. Except fury.

I had no appetite but I ate a somber meal at the hotel anyway. My mind raced into the night. When it finally calmed down I knew at least one thing: whoever had Abbie had her for a reason, and that reason was me. And what I knew. Whatever that was. I suspected - hoped - that no real harm would come to her since she was the blackmail to keep me quiet. An educated guess, anyway. One I forced myself to believe rather than the alternative.

That also meant that there would be a contact made. Soon, I hoped. I retired to our room, being sure the night clerk knew I was there. If any company were to come a-courting, I didn't want to miss them. I kept my gun close by.

Dawn came. No word. I dressed and made my way to the dining room for coffee. Sat near the front window staring out at the street. Passersby ignored me. I guess I thought someone would suddenly appear, maybe holding a sign: "Abbie is all right. Come and get her." Unlikely. Or Abbie would be there. . .I drifted off into silent thoughts.

And didn't notice the boy who stood at my elbow until he cleared his throat. Startled, I reached for the pistol on my hip. The boy stepped back, his eyes wide. I came to. Relaxed my shoulders, dropped my hand into my lap. Tried out a smile that I hadn't used in some time. The boy gulped. Handed me a piece of paper. Doffed his cap, turned on his heel and all but ran out of the café. I had intended to tip him, or at least ask him who had sent him, but he was gone before I could raise out of the chair. I opened the missal, laid it out on the table. It said:

"East on Travis Street. Nine miles. Grove behind blacksmith's shop."

Abbie awoke with a start. A noise in the shed. She had not intended to sleep but utter exhaustion had overcome her determination. How long had she slept? She could tell it was light. Another night had passed. No more trouble, she noted to herself. Someone had raised her hood enough to give her a long welcome drink of water the night before. A piece of hard bread was placed between her lips. She managed to nibble at it until she had consumed it. Another drink. The hood back down.

Rough hands took her upper arms and picked her up off the ground. She struggled but the vise grips were impossible to break. She kicked wildly but the man was quick enough to keep out of her way until she finally stopped, too tired to resist.

Half-dragged, stumbling along, Abbie and her captor made their way out of the shed and across a long path. No voices. A mockingbird took up its latest call but nothing responded. She was in the woods, perhaps.

She heard the swishing of waves at the same time she was hoisted into the air and pulled down into a boat of some kind. Maybe the same that she had been brought here in. It pushed off as she lay in its bottom. Oars working, two men huffing, she could feel the water beneath as it swept along.

A crunch as the hull struck land. Whisked quickly out of the boat and into a wagon bed. A low voice grunted "heyup" and what may have been two mules or horses - the hood kept her in the dark - lurched forward, settling into a pace and kicking up gravel on whatever road they now traveled.

Abbie lay very still, conserving her energy should an opportunity at escape present itself. Clasped gingerly in her right hand, the glass shard.

I borrowed a mount from the hotel concierge and made my way out of the city and into the plain countryside east of Houston. Travis Street quickly melted into a dirt road, but one that was wide and hard enough to be a major trade route. I traversed the miles impatiently, but did not ride hard. I needed to be cautious, prepared, and my horse ready for pursuit if necessary.

It was the middle of the morning when I spotted the smithy up and off to my left. As I approached it I could see three horses at the front post, no riders. I heard the sounds of a pounding hammer on anvil from somewhere inside in the shadows. A small barn and a corral stood just to the east of the shop, all of it weathered and worn from age and use. A gray burro stood stock still in the exact center of the small corral. Like a statue. Some chickens clucked about nearby.

I spied the grove of trees about four hundred yards behind the buildings, across an open field that lay fallow. I deliberately rode past the shop and another hundred paces without looking directly to the woods. Halted in the middle of the road. Leaned against the saddle horn, casually like I was unconcerned with the moment. But listening and watching with every inch of me. If someone was in that grove waiting for me, he - or they - would be on their own, for there was no other cover in any direction, no sign of anyone except whoever kept up the hammering inside the smith shop.

I nudged the horse left with a slight pull of the reins, and made my way across the field at an easy gait. I had my pistol on the back of my hip, a rifle slid into its pouch on the saddle. I wasn't looking for trouble. I was looking for Abbie. Trouble was looking for us.

At the edge of the cut of mesquite and live oaks I dismounted, my eyes staring hard into the shadows, the butt of the rifle inches away from the hand that held the reins as I walked forward. Ten steps, another five. There were trees behind me now, a small clearing not one hundred feet across in front of me. On the opposite end of the clearing stood three men, legs spread and braced, each man about six feet from the other. I could see the shaded outline of a wagon just to their right, two mules casually grazing.

At the same moment that I stopped, the man on my right brought a rifle up from his side and cocked it, the bullet sliding into the barrel. He pointed it straight up into the air, leaned it against his shoulder. My left hand caressed the butt of my rifle, but I left it in its sling for now. At thirty yards there was no reason for starting anything. Yet.

As I took another cautious step forward, the man standing in the middle of the trio called out in a strong voice, "That's far enough, Lincoln." I stopped. I ran through my repertoire of catchy comebacks quickly. Nothing jumped out at me, so I said nothing. "I have a message for you," he called again.

"Where's the woman?" I answered.

"She's all right."

"I want to see that for myself."

"Not going to happen," the spokesman replied firmly.

"Wrong answer," I hollered. But I waited.

"You listen to the message, you get the girl back," he said after a pause that seemed an hour long but was probably ten seconds.

"All ears," I said.

"Back off the New York case."

"If I don't?" I knew the answer, wanted to be clear.

"We start with the girl, then you, then Baker." As I thought.

I glanced at the wagon out of the corner of my eye, otherwise concentrating on the speaker and his bookend friends. A thought occurred.

"You have her here. Let her go," I said, guessing.

"You gonna walk away from this?"

"You let me and her walk away now, we walk away from this." I didn't mean it, and he probably knew it. Another thought. "Abbie?" I raised my voice.

A noise like a muffled shout came from somewhere around the wagon, high-pitched but sure. Two of the men couldn't help themselves, and turned their heads toward the sound. I glanced at the wagon, then back to the center.

"I want her out here, over here. Right now." My voice was calm, just loud enough to cross the clearing, absolute.

The two on the outside stared at the leader in the middle. He kept his eyes on me. Thirty seconds passed. No one moved. No one spoke. A crow somewhere overhead cawed as it flew by. I heard one tiny echo of the smithy's hammer. One of the mules raised its head briefly, then went back to grazing. The leader nodded his head so slightly I barely noticed, still staring between my eyes.

The man closest to the wagon back stepped to the wooden vehicle, turned and reached over the side. With some struggle he managed to lift an object up and out. Abbie landed on her feet, wrapped in a blanket, a hood over her head. Her hands were tied in front of her, her legs unbound and bare. I set my jaw.

"I'll send her to you, Lincoln," the middle man spoke once more, slowly. "You go back into town. Mind your own business. Stay out of this." I didn't say anything. He nodded imperceptibly again. His cohort walked Abbie forward, into the clearing. I took several steps forward. The man on my right let his rifle barrel down until it was pointed just above my head. I stopped.

The other guy walked Abbie to the middle of the grove, his right hand gripped on her left elbow. She tried with each step to wrestle herself from him, and each time he held on tighter. I gritted my teeth in anticipation of the next few moments. Abbie was directly between me and the spokesman now, and my attention turned to her. Her captor stopped, pulled her up straight with a jerk. I could see his face clearly now, round and fat-jowled and particularly ugly. He had a ragged smile on his face, daring me to rip it off his skull, I suppose.

We were ten paces from each other. The ugly one looked at Abbie like he was sizing up a calf at an auction, then turned back to me. In a voice that could not be heard behind him, he said to me through the grin, "She's good, ain't she?" He actually licked his lips. I didn't think someone would really do that. "Real tasty," he said for my benefit, curling the first word out of his ugly mouth.

I was deciding into which part of that face to send the first bullet, and what was sure to happen after that, when the situation was taken out of my hands. Abbie shook her wrists and the rope fell off and to the ground in a heap. In the same motion she flung her right arm in an arc that looked like a bad right cross. The ugly one made a sort of cackling, hacking sound as her hand brushed across his right cheek. Blood spurted from the slice of skin that flapped down from his cheekbone, a dark splotch that spilled down his chin and onto his shoulder. He dropped his grip on her other arm and threw both hands to his face. He spun around and began to stumble across the meadow.

The impetus of the swing threw Abbie to the ground as she followed through, and she rolled onto her side. I made a hasty decision, right or wrong, and ran the few steps to where she writhed, pulling my pistol in the same moment and pointing it generally across the clearing. With my left hand I pulled at the leather tie around her throat and she flung the hood off of her face. Her first impulse was to come after her attacker, not realizing it was me. Clawing hands reached for my eyes. I grabbed at one hand with my empty one, trying to keep my pistol up and at the real adversaries. Her free hand slapped right on my chin at the same instant she realized it was me she was flailing against. She dropped both arms to the ground.

I pulled up to one knee and wrapped both hands around the pistol. In those few seconds of distraction, the closest of the thugs had stumbled across most of the meadow. I aimed at the back of his neck, and glanced over his bent shoulders at the same time. The other two had vanished into the shadows behind where they had stood.

In my mind I pulled the trigger six times, each bullet racing through the ugly man's throat. Instead, I stood up and called for him to stop. He kept shuffling away. I had several seconds to decide his fate.

"Cale," her weak voice whispered gruffly. I looked down into her eyes. They blazed with fear and determination, but exhaustion showed all over her face. I took a deep breath. Looked up, back down into her soft eyes.

Pulled the pistol to my side. The bastard took five more steps and disappeared around a mesquite trunk, one hand still grasping at his cheek.

I knelt beside Abbie, holstering my gun but wary of any noise or movement in the glen. I put my hands on her bare shoulders and pulled her to me. Neither of us spoke for an eternity. I kissed her gently behind one ear.

"You left the place a mess," I said. She hugged me around the waist, hard.

"I wasn't expecting you back so soon," she whispered. I felt a stinging pain in the middle of my back. Reached around and touched the spot. Blood on my fingers. I frowned as I looked at it. Abbie's eyes widened slightly.

"Oh," she said. "Sorry." She brought her right hand from behind me and opened it. A piece of glass not two inches long dropped to the ground.

"You're pretty deadly with that thing," I noted. "Your friend there," I motioned with my head, "lost half his face."

"I still owe him," she said firmly, her eyes glued on mine.

I kissed her on the forehead.

"I'm starving," she said.

We took the wagon the thugs had left behind. Abbie sat on the bench with me for this trip, her arms wound tightly around me, her head against my chest. We went home.

20

Thursday, October 25, 1900 Houston

We sat together on the loveseat in our apartment, intertwined until it was hard to tell where one of us stopped and the other started. Abbie had slept for fourteen hours following a meal that a lumberjack would have choked on; I slept fitfully at best, waking every now and then to make sure she lay close beside me.

When she awoke late in the morning of the next day we made love, quietly, slowly, patiently. Discovering each other all over again. Cuts and bruises kissed and magically healed. Afterward she explained what she could of her ordeal. I was as confused as I had been since all of this – whatever the hell it was – had started.

"We have Patrick and Jones in jail on conspiracy to commit fraud and Patrick for forgery to boot," I finished updating Abbie on my New York exploits. "So why are people still after me?"

"You have such a friendly face," she noted.

"And I'm socially acceptable," I agreed.

"Maybe they're jealous."

"Who wouldn't be?"

"Maybe you've offended someone," she offered.

"Who me?" I asked. "The model of congeniality?"

"You have your moments."

"You seem to enjoy some of them," I said.

"Some of them are wondrous," she agreed.

"I feel one of those very moments even as we speak." I generally did when she was within a hundred miles of me.

"I would hate to miss any of those," she whispered in my ear ever so softly.

It was a wondrous moment.

"I have to go back to New York," I said an hour or so later as we lay together in the bathtub. It had four gold-flaked legs, very ornate, and plumbing to match.

"I know," she said in a quiet, uneasy voice.

"You could come with me this time," I offered.

"I'd like that," she replied. "As long as I won't be in the way of your investigation." She turned her head and looked up into my eyes. I grimaced.

"I will find a way to work around you."

"If it becomes cold I can keep you warm."

"An offer I would never refuse," I said. "The bath water is cooling down, in fact." Abbie smiled up at me.

We went to New York.

The train ride, this time, was uneventful. Abbie and I actually enjoyed the journey together, watching as the landscapes sped by, state after state. Rolling hills and wide rivers, towns of every shape and size, people waving at stations, all the world made up of strangers except for the two of us. I had paid little attention on my last round trip to the East. The weather turned progressively colder as we made our way up through Pennsylvania, then New Jersey and into the city. As we stepped from the Pullman onto the ramp at Grand Central Station, a pounding noise coming from the roof warned that a driving rainstorm would soon greet us.

It was Monday morning, October 29.

Captain Jim Baker had been very busy while I was gone. He and Detective Vallely had made the rounds of all the suspects, several times. Albert Patrick would defend himself. John R. Potts had been retained by Charlie Jones. I didn't recognize the name at first, but later recalled that Potts officed in the same suites at the Broadway Chambers Building as Patrick. Cozy.

Three other attorneys, Baker reported to me on Monday evening, had also been questioned. Morris Meyers was a partner with Patrick, shifty-eyed and uneasy during the interrogation. Thomas W. Ford was a lawyer originally from Texas who had been working with Patrick just since August. Any connection to Texas interested me. And last, Orren T. Holt had also been asked about his knowledge of the last will of William Marsh Rice. Holt had helped draft and file the controversial last will of Rice's second wife.

"We're still working on that case in the courts," Baker was saying as we sat in Vallely's cubicle. "Damned if I'm going to give up on that one, even if Mr. Rice is gone. We'll beat it." I nodded. "Anyway," Baker continued, "Holt swears he had nothing to do with the Rice will, and we've got exactly nothing to impeach that."

"But he does have a connection," I said.

"Damned straight he does," Vallely broke in. "He knows a helluva lot more than he's telling."

"And we'll get it," Baker took back up again. "It'll take some time, but we'll get it."

"And you said you heard from the coroner?" I asked.

"Yes," said Baker. "Saturday afternoon. Bob Aurich came by to see me, the report fresh in his hands. You wanna take a guess what they found inside the old man?"

"Bananas?" I ventured.

"Chloroform," Baker grinned like the Cheshire. "Just a trace in his lungs and throat, but enough." He paused, for dramatic effect. "And?"

"Bananas?" I was guessing again.

"Mercury," Baker said *sotto voce*. "Enough to kill a horse."

"Enough to kill Rice?"

"Actually, the coroner was less enthused," Baker admitted. "Said that mercury pills had been ingested over a long period of time. Said lots of people use the pills for all sorts of ailments. Especially the old folks."

"Does it work? Make 'em well, that is?"

"He said it wasn't good for much, no."

"So it may have killed Rice?"

"Maybe was as strong as the coroner would go. Not enough for a judge."

"Mercury pills," I said it as a statement I was mulling over.

"Went back to the old man's apartment. Found an empty pill bottle. The coroner has it right now."

"You expect he'll find traces of mercury in it?"

"Right." Baker sat back in his chair, finished with his summary.

"Okay," I said after a moment of silence among the three of us. "What's next?"

"We go back to Patrick and Jones. Again. Put a shoulder into 'em," Vallely offered. He probably meant that literally.

"You think they'll fold this time?" I asked. "Or the next?"

"I've got time," said the detective, tightening his fists at his side.

"We get Patrick on forgery, Jones on murder?" I was thinking way ahead of the conversation. There was still something missing. If any of the attacks on me were related to this case, who was behind it and why were they still after me? We had our two suspects behind bars, enough to put them away for awhile, maybe Jones forever.

But I wanted Patrick. Jones was a patsy, a puppet. Too easy to take him down. He didn't mastermind any of this. It had to be Patrick, or someone behind him maybe. A forgery conviction in New York would get him a year up at Ossining, max. Then he was out and gone. That wasn't good enough for me or Baker or Vallely.

But taking on Patrick directly wouldn't work either. Too cool a customer, which was why I wanted to see him swing. So Jones wasn't the end, but he might be the means.

"We have to get Jones to roll on Patrick," Baker said, thinking down the same path as me.

"I agree," I said.

"What do we have to work with?"

"The chloroform, for starters," I said. "We put the chloroform in Jones' hand, force him to put the conspiracy on Patrick or whoever sent him after Rice that night."

"And if he doesn't 'fess up?" Vallely interjected.

"He will," I said. "There's a key here somewhere. We're staring right at it and don't see it. And it may be that I have the key. That's why they're after me." The other two men raised eyebrows in tandem. I told them about the attack on the train, about Abbie being kidnapped. They listened, hardly breathing. When I finished, Vallely snorted.

"You got nobody in jail for that? No bodies? No identification? No damn nothing?" He didn't seem pleased that I was at least still alive.

"Never mind that," Baker spoke up. "You're right, Cale. Somebody's after you, needs you quiet. What have you got?" He stared up at the ceiling.

"I can't put my finger on it, Captain. It's right here, I feel it. There's just one small piece missing." I was as frustrated as the others. More so.

"We'll find it. In the meantime, you watch your back and we will, too. Detective, will you put a man on Lincoln while he's in the city?"

"Yeah," Vallely cleared his throat. "Sure."

"Gosh, thanks, Officer," I beamed. He snorted an obscenity. I turned to Baker. "I want to talk to Jones and Patrick again."

"No problem. They're locked up neat and tidy in the Tombs. Say when."

"Day after tomorrow," I said after a moment to think. "I want to go back to the apartment first. And I want to talk to Patrick's law firm associates."

"We'll set it up for tomorrow. Meet you at 500 Madison at ten."

We searched Rice's apartment from top to bottom. I walked the hallway a dozen times, paced the distance from Jones' bedroom to the master, to the bathroom and the kitchen, where one might dispose of evidence down sinks. I opened and closed doors, peeked out windows and under beds, behind cupboards and looked for secret compartments. Nothing.

After lunch at a dark café over on Broadway we headed down to the two hundred block, then to the thirteenth floor of the Chambers building where Patrick's name still appeared across a glass door. I noted the other names below it, in smaller type. Meyers. Potts. Short.

Baker and I walked inside. No secretary was there to meet us. I pushed open the office door to our right. A man in a dark blue suit stood up from behind a desk. He moved very slowly, gingerly, as if nursing some pain somewhere. A large swatch of bandage covered one side of his face. He'd been into something, and appeared to have lost. A bell went off somewhere inside me.

"May I help you gentlemen?" He had a squeaky voice, pitiful.

"We need to speak to Mr. Patrick's law associates," Baker said in his most courteous but business-like voice.

"I am John R. Potts, attorney at law, and at your service," the recuperating lawyer replied by rote. "The police have interviewed me several times. What more do you want?"

"I'm James Baker, of Baker and Botts in Houston," the captain strode forward to within reach of his prey. "I visited with you once before myself, if you'll recall."

"Yes, uh, yes, of course," said Potts. "And?" He looked at me. Then he did an interesting thing: he blinked. Not once but three or four times. His shoulders pulled back and his eyes started shifting around, looking at everything except me.

"This is Pinkerton Detective Caleb Lincoln of Galveston," Baker formally introduced me. I smiled my very best smile. Potts barely nodded. Blinked twice more.

And I knew why in that next moment.

"We've met before," I said calmly.

"Oh?" Potts whispered as it caught in his throat.

"On the train," I said in a very, very quiet, steady tone.

"Why, I haven't been to Houston in two years. Nor have I been on a train this year to anywhere. Nor do I remember you, sir." Potts sort of grunted. Too many nors.

"Captain, did I say anything about the train being bound for Houston?" I kept my eyes glued on Potts' forehead.

"Why, no, Mr. Lincoln, you didn't." His eyes trained on Potts.

"Well, er, you said you were from Galveston," Potts stammered. "I just assumed -" his voice trailed off.

"You've been injured recently, I see," I continued. I had him. "That damage to your face: what could have caused such a thing?"

"It's none of your business," Potts said, "but I don't mind telling you: the door to this building slammed on me when the wind was high several days ago."

"Looks more like a china plate from a dining car, if you ask me." I didn't wait for Potts to deny it. "And your other injuries likely from a swift kick? Perhaps a pounding into the floor?" Potts stared blankly. "Who was it dragged you out of there, Potts? Did you two hide on the train? Jump off?" I was talking faster. Baker was now staring at me, the realization coming.

"It was Meyers," Potts suddenly blurted out. "He made me get on that train. He had a gun. He was going to kill you. I didn't have anything to do with it." Potts was whimpering. Made me want to slap him silly.

"Who gave the orders?" Baker asked. "Was it Patrick?"

"I don't know," Potts blubbered, rubbing the back of his neck and shaking his head. "Morris told me to go with him. Said he had a job to do."

"Bad job," I noted.

"Look, Mr. Lincoln," Potts was coming around from behind his desk, his shoulders sagging. I thought for a moment he was going to get down on his knees. "Please keep me out of this. I was just going along. I don't know who was in charge. I don't know why we, uhm, they were after you -"

I slapped him silly.

We found Morris Meyers two hours later in a tavern off Broadway. He was tight-lipped when we arrested him. He and Potts spent that night in jail. We had them on assault, but that wouldn't help us get Patrick.

It was time to go see Patrick and Jones.

Wednesday morning, October 31. The Tombs State Prison, second floor.

I sat in a spacious jail cell alone with Albert T. Patrick, attorney, conspirator, and, I was pretty sure, murderer. I sat in an ancient straight back chair. The inmate sat on his cot, his legs and arms crossed comfortably, like we were sitting in his den in front of a roaring fire. He had an amiable look on his face, like we were best friends. A tray of emptied breakfast dishes sat on the floor by the door. The conversation was not going anywhere, and fast.

"I am astonished that Mr. Potts would drag my name into this situation," Patrick was saying in a surprised tenor. "I assure you, Detective, that I know nothing of this attempt on your life. Why would I be at all interested in such a thing?"

"Perhaps because I know enough to put you away for the rest of your life?"

"Oh? What is it you know, Mr. Lincoln?"

"I know that Mr. Rice's will is a forgery, that you and he never worked together. May have not even have known each other. I know that you got restless when the old man didn't die over the summer. You wanted to skim off his estate, which you could do as executor of that will. I know that you enticed Charlie Jones into the plan because he was next to Rice twenty-four hours a day, because he had Rice's trust.

"I know you had Jones administer mercury in pills to Mr. Rice for weeks, maybe months, hoping to kill the old man with a gradual overdose." I had rehearsed this speech a thousand times to myself. "I know you became impatient when nothing was happening," I went on with what I did know, filling in the blanks with educated guesses. Patrick didn't blink.

"I know you decided to hurry up the process sometime in September. You got hold of a bottle of chloroform and gave instructions to Jones to administer it while Rice slept that night."

"Mercury tablets are illegal in the State of New York, Mr. Lincoln," Patrick interjected. "If I had done such a thing - which I did not - how could I get hold of the chemical?" We stared at each other for a moment. A pause.

"From Texas," I heard myself say. Patrick raised an eyebrow. "You ordered it from someone you knew back in Texas."

The puzzle was suddenly coming together as I listened to myself work through it. Everything falling in place in a heartbeat. The key, the lock snapping open.

"Fascinating!" Patrick was mewing, all smiles. "Bravo! Great detective work! And what proof do you have, may I ask? Documentation? Postage records? A delivery receipt, perhaps, to my address?" He knew I had none of these.

"I'll get it," I said firmly.

"Oh, I don't think so, Detective. Because there is nothing to your theory, albeit interesting. Worthy of a novella, I might add. But you'll have to leave me out of it, I'm afraid. I simply do not fit into your puzzle." He smiled disingenuously. Ripping that smile from his jaws was tempting. I refrained.

"Someone else knows, Patrick," I assured him. "We'll make the connection."

"Ah, Mr. Lincoln, I do so admire your persistence. But I think our conversation must come to an end. I have my exercise hour coming soon, a walk in the yard. You'll please excuse me." He stood up from his cot and extended a hand which I ignored. I headed out of the cell and down the dank corridor.

"Please come back when you have another delightful story to share," he called after me.

I sprinted upstairs to the third floor cell where Charlie Jones sat shivering in fear, not from the cold. When he saw me at the door his eyes brightened momentarily, thinking someone had paid bail for his release. When he recognized me, he slumped back into the corner, looked away as I walked in.

"Charlie," I said gently, "you and I need to talk again." I sat in a chair equally ancient from the previous quarters. He did not acknowledge my presence. I spoke carefully, quietly. "I've been with Patrick. I know he's the one behind Mr. Rice's murder. I know you were just his puppet, acting out for him. He has something over you, Charlie, and it's scaring the hell out of you. But you don't have to be scared of him anymore." At that, Jones turned his head halfway in my direction. "He's locked up forever. We've got him. He can never hurt you again." I was bluffing.

"Yes he will," in a whisper. "Yes he will."

"No, Charlie. If you will help me, we can put him away. He's the murderer, he's the conspirator. A jury will see that. But you have to help us here, Charlie." I waited. Nothing. I tried again. "Where did you get the mercury pills? Where did you get the chloroform? Who told you how to suffocate Mr. Rice?" No response. "It was Patrick, wasn't it, Charlie?" An eternity went by in silence. Then,

"He'll track me down. He'll kill me. Him or one of his goons. They'll kill me, that's all." Charlie was shaking.

"We can get you out of here, out of New York." I was reaching. "We can get you back to your family in Texas." His eyes met mine for the first time. "You can be with your father and your brothers -"

"No!" Charlie's voice was sharp and angry in an instant. Then he put his head in his hands and began to sob.

"What's the matter, Charlie? Why can't you be with your family?" I was stepping through that unlocked door.

"Dead," he said.

"Your family's dead?"

He shook his head. "My brother Franklin. They told me he's dead. He was my best friend, and now he's dead."

"What happened?"

"The hurricane," Charlie answered between sobs. "He died in the hurricane last month. My father wired me last week that the sheriff had told him."

"I'm sorry about your brother," I said and meant it. But I knew now. "Lots of people died that weekend," I said. "Thousands. I was there. I was in it. It was terrible, Charlie. A terrible tragedy for you and so many others." I sat back. Charlie cried.

And now it was all there. What I knew that I didn't know I knew. Until now. Why they were after me. The last piece of the puzzle. I leaned forward.

"What was your brother's name?"

"Frank."

"That his whole name?" I mentally crossed my fingers. Be right.

"Father liked to give his boys big names, important names, names we could live up to, I guess." He sniffled, rubbed the back of one hand across the bridge of his nose. "Benjamin Franklin Jones," he announced. "I called him Frank."

On that slip of paper, that prescription: *Ben Jones*.

I wasn't so sure now that I wanted to be right. But I was. Oh, brother.

"Charlie," I said. "Your brother Franklin died in the storm, all right, but he didn't die because of the storm." Jones looked up at me, tears staining his reddened face. "Someone shot him,

Charlie. Killed him because of what he knew." I let that sink in. I pictured the stairwell of Gresham's house, the body falling, the blood on the back of his neck, the crowd gasping when I told them. Charlie was holding his breath, waiting. I started again.

"It was your brother who sent you the mercury pills, wasn't it? Your brother had connections down in Texas. He could get that for you, no questions asked, no records, no one else would know. He was your best friend, you could count on him, trust him. He didn't even ask you what it was for, did he, Charlie?" Jones slowly shook his head.

"But someone found out, someone else knew. And there was only one person who could know, right, Charlie?" Only the one who was behind all of it: the will, the murder, the estate. "And who was that, Charlie?" I stopped.

After a minute had plodded by in silence, Charlie looked up at me.

"I didn't want to do it," he said, his voice choking and cracking. "He made me do it. Said the old man was dying anyway, why not hurry it along. 'Put him out of his misery,' he said. The mercury was taking too long. Mr. Rice was going to give all of his money away to the Institute. There'd be nothing left, not for anyone. Not for me. I worked for Mr. Rice, day and night. Never got a thank you, never got a raise. He said I would be rich. I could live anywhere I wanted." Charlie straightened his shoulders.

"I didn't really want all that money," he continued. "I just wanted some respect, some thanks. Is that too much to ask?" I shook my head, encouraging him to go on. "He told me we could do it, him and me. Nobody would ever figure it out. Old men die every day. Mr. Rice was sick, that's what we'd tell everyone. I was scared of him. He told me I would be stupid to pass up this opportunity. That he'd find a way without me and blame it on me if he got caught. Said this was the only way it would work so we'd both be rich." Charlie stopped. Caught his breath.

"Who was it, Charlie?" I asked again. He gulped.

"Mr. Patrick. Albert Patrick." Pause. "Did he kill my brother?"

"He had it done, Charlie," I replied. "Your brother knew too much. The storm was a perfect moment. It was Patrick's good luck, that's all, to have a cover for the murder. But it didn't turn out that way. I couldn't make the connection, until just now, that the murdered man was your brother." I reached over and patted Charlie Jones on the shoulder.

"Now we'll get him," I said.

I called for the jailer. We got Vallely and Baker there in two hours. When I headed for the hotel and Abbie that evening, I left Charlie Jones writing a confession implicating Albert Patrick in the murder of William Marsh Rice.

Got him.

Part Four

Beaumont, Texas
Eight Weeks Later

21

I met Peck Byrd on the 20th of December. He had come into Houston looking for a security guard at his work site in Beaumont. Next to loving Abbie, security guard was what I knew best. Someone must've told someone, and so on, because he came knocking at my door.

"Gonna need security for a couple of weeks over the holidays," he explained to me. I was interested. I liked Peck the moment we met. "Our crew's takin' off on Christmas Eve, gonna be back to work after the First. Pay's pretty good, living quarters pretty bad." I've taken worse offers.

"Any particular kind of trouble you expecting?" I inquired. Not that it mattered.

"Not really. Just a lot of equipment needs looking after. Could be some pranksters might try to rough the site up, could cause a lot of damage, slow us up," he said.

"You want me twenty-four hours?"

"More or less, uh huh."

"Sounds good to me. You want me there before the 24th?"

"If you can," Peck replied. "We lost one of our crew, guy named McLeod, the other day. Kinda short-handed right now. If you don't mind a little roughneck work, there's some extra pay in it for you."

"Roughneck?" I asked.

"Working a drilling rig," Byrd explained. "Captain Lucas is drilling for oil south of Beaumont on Big Hill. Thinks we're on to something."

"Never done rig work," I admitted.

"Most haven't," Peck smiled. "'Less you're from Pennsylvania," he added.

"Nope. Got roughed up there once passing through, is all."

"Well, it's rough damn work, but we could use ya," he said.

I turned to Abbie who was sitting across the room on the loveseat, half-listening. And back to the man standing in front of me.

"Sounds like a good enough deal," I said, sticking my hand out. We shook. "I'll see you in two days."

"You'll be careful," she said after Byrd had left, her arms around my waist and her face close to mine.

"As ever," I whispered.

"That's not comforting."

"I'm learning how each time," I said.

"Slowly," she observed.

"Yes. But it tends to sink in better that way."

"I see." She wasn't comforted.

I stepped off the train at the Beaumont depot on Tuesday Noon, December 22nd. The streets of the river town were quiet, but the place was clean and neat, the dirt roads crisscrossing for several blocks. I noted a boardinghouse or two, a bar, three or four restaurants, a livery and a bank, two churches, almost all of them on the main street I walked. I was nearly alone. The few folks I saw nodded pleasantly to me.

I walked into a small one-story building at the south end of town, put a dollar down for two weeks rent of a small, tidy bedroom located in the back of the store where Peck Byrd had directed me. Unpacked my one bag, hitched my gun on my hip, and went down to see Big Hill.

I was not impressed. It was actually no more than a rise on the landscape, west of the river, a mile or so south from the last buildings of Beaumont. Off to one side stood some fir trees. They looked out of place, and one of them had a funny tip on it, sort of bent over. The rest was scrub brush, high plains grass. Just off the crest – that was an exaggeration – I could see the outline of the rig, the only thing that rose more than ten feet off the ground in most any direction.

The rig itself was makeshift at best. It looked like it might withstand a hefty storm but maybe not for long. I figured it was maybe forty feet high, wider at the bottom where a plank platform bolstered it. In the center the drilling pipe disappeared into a hole and headed for oil or China or wherever they were going.

Several men were scurrying around on the platform. Two men stood talking about fifty feet away. One was outfitted for work, the other in a suit. The suit was pointing, gesturing, and the other man was nodding his head in response. I headed for the pair, figuring one of them was in charge. A voice hailed me as I circled around the platform. I looked up and waved at Peck who was ten feet off the ground climbing onto the scaffold. The pair to the side noticed me coming in their direction, and took several steps to meet me.

"Caleb Lincoln," I said as I shook their extended hands.

"I'm Al Hamill," the roughneck introduced himself. "Glad to meet ya. Peck's been talking about you coming. This here's Captain Anthony Lucas." I nodded again to the man in the suit.

"My pleasure, Mr. Lincoln," he said with a noticeable German accent.

"Cale," I corrected him.

"Cale it is," Lucas said. "Good of you to come on short notice. We'll need someone to watch the rig for a couple of weeks."

"Peck said you might could use some help for a day or two on the rig."

"Yep," Hamill spoke up. "We're a man short, and having a devil of a time getting anybody from town to come out here."

"Any particular reason?" I asked.

"Nah," Hamill grinned. "Work's too hard, that's all."

"And it may be they don't believe in what we're doing out here," added Lucas.

"You mean the oil?" Nothing if not sharp.

"Sure thing," said Hamill. "We're near eight hundred feet right now, hardly a spit so far. Tough drilling, more granite than sand." Made no sense to me, but I listened politely. "My brother and I" – he motioned toward the crew – "we come down from Corsicana when Mr. Walter Sharp needed this rig built. Oil up there, but not much. Mostly water wells. All of 'em shallow." He was talking to himself now. "Not like this one," he said, staring at the top of the rig with an odd, bemused expression.

"Eight hundred feet pretty deep?" Mama said you wouldn't learn if you didn't ask.

"Nothing like it in these United States," Hamill responded matter of fact.

"Twice as deep as most, Mr. Lincoln," Lucas added. "You'd have to go to Russia to find anything like this one."

"No thanks," I said. "This one'll be just fine." Hamill chuckled.

I worked two days on the rig, fourteen hours each day, work about as hard as anything I'd ever done. I liked Curt Hamill as much as his brother and the captain. Fine folks, hard workers, kept an eye on each other all the time, seemed to know their business. The drilling was slow going, interrupted constantly by little problems. A loose pipe, a call for more mud sluiced down into the hole. The noise of the pump and the pipe, the squeaking of the tower, all kind of melted together after awhile.

Once or twice I noticed some boys come to watch. They were probably no more than twelve years old, sitting on their ponies. Just watching. They'd sit there for twenty minutes or so, then ride off down the hill. Come back a few hours later.

On the afternoon of the 24th I met Pattillo Higgins. He rode out from town in a one-horse rig, rode up slowly as he gazed up and down the tower. He had a tall, gray ten-*galon* hat that he wore perched right on top of his head. His suit coat was pinned in the middle of the left sleeve where his arm stopped right where the elbow should have been. He thrust his good right arm out to me when we met.

"Mr. Higgins is the one who got all this started," Al Hamill explained to me after the introductions. "Been a Beaumonter near all his life, isn't that right, Pattillo?" The gentleman nodded. "Walked this hill a thousand times, was the only one who thought there might be something of value on it. Or below it, that is."

"Salt dome underneath," Higgins said, like it should mean something to me. I smiled.

"Yeah," Hamill continued. "It's a reach but that's what we're here to find out, if it's true. Anyhow, Mr. Higgins finally convinced some men who put money behind this deal. And he got Captain Lucas down here from Pennsylvania. He even got John Galey to look it over." John Galey, I thought. Nope.

"Mr. Lincoln," Higgins finished the story for my benefit, "I am confident that somewhere down there," he looked to the ground, "we'll find petroleum. I'm sure of it. A thousand feet, it's there. Mr. Galey has brought in the best there is. Walter Sharp and his brother Jim are part of this enterprise, Captain Lucas is the best engineer on the continent. And the Hamill boys – well, there's no one better at drilling."

"But not this week," Hamill said. "We finish up here in two hours. Mr. Galey wants us home with our families for the holidays. We'll be back around the 2nd. Meantime, Cale, she's all yours."

I'd had the dream for three or four nights now. Teddy was hollering in his high-pitched voice for us to get off our asses and get up Kettle Hill. The

Spanish artillery was hitting us hard from above and there was no sense laying in the trenches to die. May as well die fighting for the hill.

Even in my dream it was hot and muggy, mosquitoes and flies all over me as I worked my way up the hill. There was almost no infantry to fight, just snipers mostly. Bullets whizzed by me as I stumbled along at Roosevelt's side. He never looked back, never even winced when the explosions went off or the guns belched. Just kept walking up that damn hill, right up the trail. It was like he couldn't be hit, someone watching over him. Whatever. I stayed close to him.

As the dream unfolded, we made the crest of the hill at last and it all looked like Big Hill now, with oil rigs spotted everywhere. Men shooting at us from the tops of the towers. Soldiers scattering, falling. Teddy and I headed for the biggest rig set dead center on the crest. A five-pounder blew grapeshot all around us. A soldier to my left disappeared in a mass of blood and tissue and bone, like a watermelon when you hit it with a shotgun blast.

We make the crest, we make a last dash to the massive rig, Teddy and I leap onto the platform in the same instant.

A man is sitting at a rickety desk, pen in hand. He's writing something on a parchment. He looks up at me. It's Charlie Jones, but he has no eyes. The sockets are empty, black. White streaks run down his face. Teddy is gone. The battle is over. Charlie stands up from his seat, pulls a knife from his back pocket. As the hollow face stares right through me, the knife slices across a wrist. His hand falls to the ground. I look *down. My left arm is severed in the same moment, dropping onto the bed —*

I awoke in a sweat, grabbing for my arm which had gone numb where I slept on it. I sat up on the side of the cot in the little room.

Cheap whiskey, I reminded myself. Gotta remember that.

I worked the rig security for ten days, no trouble. Had several long, extended visits with Captain Lucas and also with Higgins. Both men kind of quirky about some things, like oil for one, but both were absolutely determined to succeed. Both of them believed in what they were doing. I liked that about them.

On the 2nd of January the crew returned and was immediately back at work. I agreed to stay on and help for awhile, although I did make a quick overnight trip to be with Abbie in Houston. She wanted to come to Beaumont with me but there really wasn't anything for her to do there at the moment; I promised I'd bring her over in a week or so if I was still there.

I had telegrams from Captain Baker who had returned to New York City to make sure the trial was on schedule. Albert Patrick had been indicted on charges from conspiracy to commit fraud to forging the will to conspiracy to commit murder. The grand jury had balked at first degree murder, but we had enough to put him away without it. Charlie Jones was up for his part in

Mr. Rice's death, but his signed confession might help his case some.

Charlie was also on what they called suicide watch at the Tombs. The night he had confessed to me he tried to kill himself in his jail cell. Cut his wrists.

The trial was still weeks away. I thought I could probably work here on Big Hill until Baker called me, then head back to New York to give whatever testimony might be of help to the DA.

Everything seemed to be in order. But I knew that everything was not settled. We had Patrick and Jones behind bars. Meyers and Potts would soon go on trial for their part in the conspiracy to forge Rice's will. They didn't have enough to put them up for assault. David Short had played a part in it, too, taking the check to the bank the morning after Rice died. But he would probably get off.

But someone was still out there and I wanted him. The red-haired man who had killed Ben Jones in Galveston and damn near killed me, he was still unaccounted for. He'd set fire to the warehouse with me in it, sent thugs after me and kidnapped Abbie. I owed him for each of those, especially the last.

But his identity was still a mystery. And what was the connection? No confessions, no evidence, no identification, no damn nothing as Vallely would say. I had stared into men's faces as I walked the Houston streets all November, thinking I might come upon him. He haunted my dreams when it wasn't Charlie Jones trying to kill himself. It was as close as I was getting, and it was damn frustrating.

It was a beautiful sunset this Thursday evening. The temperature was hovering around freezing, had been for a week. The skies were clear and the breeze was cold. I walked back into town alone, exhausted from another long shift on the rig.

It had been a bad week for the Hamills and their crew. The hole was down to a thousand feet, twenty lengths of fifty-foot pipes screwed together and pumping the drill bit against quicksand and rock and whatever the hell else was down there. We'd brought up some strange stuff earlier, turned out to be sulphur. We'd hit some gas pockets along the way, too, which always scared the hell out of us. The pipes would slip a few feet as if they'd hit an opening, then there'd be a hissing sound and something like firecrackers echoing up from below. We had about ten seconds to get the hell off the platform before the gas blew out. Somebody'd shout, we'd drop and run.

Nothing much came from those, just a little excitement stirred into the constant toil.

And no oil. Oh, there'd been some signs here and there, piddling amounts slewing off into the pit. But never enough to get anybody excited. Lucas would sit on his haunches beside the pit, letting the spillage filter through his fingers. He'd smell it, taste it, rub it in the palm of his hand, then wipe it off and walk away. Each time he would walk about a hundred yards from the platform, jam both hands deep into his pants pockets and stare off toward the horizon, his thoughts his own.

Now the pipe was jamming almost every day. Lucas thought we'd gotten into a fissure below the salt dome, and it was steering the bit crooked. If the bit broke off down there – they'd lost a couple already – it meant pulling all the pipe, waiting until another bit could be brought down from Corsicana, and starting all over again.

And time was money. Mr. Galey had a lot of money but not what he wanted to spend on this one hole, especially if it was going to come up dry. There was a lot of believing going on, but it wasn't going to hold the operation together forever. Gladys City Oil and Gas, that's what Higgins had named the operation after some little girl in his Sunday School class, was on a deadline.

Thursday Noon, January 9 Beaumont
I had just finished lunch with Captain Lucas and his wife at their modest home near Big Hill. Mrs. Lucas was quite a cook and a terrific lady, right in the thick of things, knew all about oil and

drilling, believed in what her husband believed, never complained about the living conditions they had there. Someone had said she kept the operation going earlier when everyone else was ready to give up. Had told John Galey that there *was* oil there, that he shouldn't back out now, and had flat talked him into staying with the project. Strong.

A boy came barreling down the dirt trail, hopped onto the front porch, pulled his cap off his head and in a breathy voice announced that he had an urgent telegram for Mr. Caleb Lincoln. He flailed it in the air in front of him for effect. I flipped a coin in his direction that I had drug from a pocket. He caught it in his hat, reminding me of the messenger who had come to my hotel room way back whenever. Maybe they get trained to do that. He beamed a smile at me and took off running back to town.

JANUARY 9, NEW YORK CITY
TO DETECTIVE CALEB LINCOLN, HOUSTON
URGENT

BREAK IN TEXAS CASE. COLEMAN AND LEE IMPLICATED. NEED THE HIRED GUN TO FINISH INVESTIGATION. LAST PIECE OF PUZZLE. ANY LEADS?
BAKER

I recognized the names. Coleman and Lee had been suspects in the Rice conspiracy because of their connections to Patrick and Jones here in Texas. It had been a thin thread, but obviously somebody had kept at it.

"The hired gun" was my nemesis, my nightmare. Whatever he had, whoever he was, I needed to track him down. If he was the only one left, he was for sure now the other murderer. I had seen him that night at the Gresham house, just a glance, looking down at me among the crowd on the balconies above. He was the one who killed Ben Jones. He had vanished then, and every other time I'd come close. He was a phantom. No one ever remembered him or could identify him. I couldn't have told anyone how tall or wide he was myself. No name. An apparition, a ghost.

And I had to find him. It was personal now.

22

I caught the afternoon train back into Houston, arriving there around 5:00 and in time to take Abbie out for dinner. I caught her up on what had happened. She knew about the telegram because it had been delivered to the hotel room. She was expecting me.

"So what do you do now," she asked over our after-dinner coffee.

"Don't know," I said because I didn't have the slightest notion. "Thought I would go down to the police station in a few minutes, see what they have on this end. Anything new. It's been a couple of months."

"Maybe 'your man' will be in jail," she said.

"And his written confession posted on the precinct board, and a party in my honor under way," I added.

"If he thinks you are after him, he'll try to kill you again."

"Yes."

"I wouldn't like that."

"If he tries I will prevail." I wanted to sound assured.

"I don't want to lose you. Not now."

"I will not let that happen, Abbie," I said. "But," I added, "if he doesn't come after me we lose him. I am the only thing that can bring him out of hiding. If he thinks I know what connects him to this case, he'll have to stop me."

"He hires thugs," she said, making the word actually sound genteel somehow.

"His thugs do not concern me."

"So you will make yourself the bait."

"It is a plan."

"I don't much care for it."

"It is not my favorite plan," I admitted. "But it will work."

"And I shall sit here in the hotel and wring my hands and wait for you to come back dead or alive."

"No. You will be under protective care of the finest Houston detective agency, and not in this hotel. For now."

"If you think that is best."

"Abbie, I need to not worry about you. I have to get this guy, not only to finish the case, but for me. For you and me. He will always be out there unless I finish this. Besides, I owe him."

"I will still wring my hands," she finally replied after a moment.

"No one does that better. Everyone will talk about it." She smiled, barely.

March 4, 1877, Washington, D.C. The twelve-year-old boy had been drawn to the noise of the gathering crowd two blocks from the alleyway where he slept, and mostly lived. It was midday and hundreds of people were jostling their way down the street toward the capitol building steps. A podium was set up there and police and soldiers stood around in the vicinity. Flags flew from poles that had been put up the day before. A band struck up a tune and some people cheered.

The boy walked alone in the midst of the congregation until he was only a few yards from the podium. He stared up into people's faces but no one returned his gaze. Then a louder cheer went up and a man leading an entourage of a dozen or so made their way down the concrete steps until he stood behind the podium. He waved and smiled at the crowds.

As the boy watched, perplexed at the occasion but riveted on the activity, another man strode up to the waving one. The two men shook hands. The crowd went silent. A book was picked up off the podium and the second man held it while the first put his hand on it and raised his other. There was some mumbling that the boy couldn't make out. Then another hurrah from the crowd. More smiling and waving.

The man began to speak. He spoke for fifteen minutes, interrupted several times by the throng. He didn't seem to mind. When he was done he shoved the papers from his speech into a breast pocket, waved some more to the crowd and, now joined by a woman who appeared to be his wife, walked back up the steps and disappeared into the huge, white building.

The crowd began to filter out of the square. The boy stayed a moment longer in wonderment at all the fanfare. He overheard someone mention that this man "would make a fine president now." The boy wondered if someone might kill him like Mr. Lincoln.

The twelve year old wandered to the edge of the square and into a small park. Three men stood in a small group off to one side in the limited shade of an old maple tree. They were hard into a conversation, very agitated, frowning. The boy edged in their direction to listen. The men did not notice; if they did they ignored his presence. One of them was speaking in a hushed but angry voice.

"Hayes is a damned nigger-lover," he was spitting the words out one at a time like they were dirt clods. "Another goddamned black republican like the others." The boy didn't think that the man he had just watched was black, not even a little bit. He kept listening.

"Well, boys, we've been quiet long enough. It's our time again. No nigger's gonna vote while I've got a breath in me." The others mumbled in agreement. "We'll get our country back if it's the last thing we do." More mumbling. "Mebbe Mr. Goddamn Hayes needs what Abe damn Lincoln got: a bullet in his brain."

That was all the boy could stand. He felt the shudder again, remembering when his mother had died right before his eyes, dragged and beaten *until she stopped breathing. Remembered the white robes, the torches, the shouts.*

Reached down to the ground, picked up a fallen limb about four feet long and an inch thick. Took three steps toward the trio until he was only another step away. Said in his hardest voice: "This is for Mr. Lincoln and my Mama." Swung the limb in a long arc with both hands gripping it at arms' length, his weight lifting off his back leg and into the strike. The tip of the limb caught the one who had been talking flush in the mouth, just on his upper lip. Blood and cartilage and teeth exploded from his face in an instant as the limb broke into two uneven pieces. The man grabbed his head with both hands as an unearthly howl spewed from his broken jaws. The other two stood frozen. The boy ran.

The Houston police had no leads, no new information, on the man who killed Benjamin Franklin Jones. With Galveston still mopping up, and the toll of dead now past the four thousand mark, that crime and others had been shifted to other cities that could handle them for now. I filled them in on what information I had - the connection with Rice and Patrick's allies in Texas - but an hour's conversation resulted in another impasse. All the trails were cold.

I thanked the men for their cooperation thus far, we promised each other we'd stay in touch and especially if any new developments arose, a round of shaking hands, and I left.

Outside it was blustery cold, the wind whipping through the city streets with a vengeance all its own. I could see stars above me, and the promise of a very cold morning coming. It was only a few blocks to the Rice Hotel and I waved off two hacks because I needed the brisk walk to think. It must have been after eight o'clock.

I spotted my shadow when I turned a corner and happened to look over my shoulder. He was seventy-five yards behind me and across the street, wandering through deep shadows under the building awnings. In the instant my eyes made him he made the mistake of turning to look in a store window. Idiot. Window shopping in the dark, looking into a pitch-black shop? Well, that's one way to save money, I thought as I rambled after him. No sense heading on to the hotel. Let's get this taken care of right now.

He waited only long enough to realize I was coming right after him. Broke and ran. He was not fast and I was. He rounded a corner and when I got there I lost him for a brief second. There he was. He'd crossed the street. I followed. He ducked into an alley at full speed, and nearly lost his balance. I was making up the distance with each stride. I hit the alley at full speed myself, assuming he wouldn't be waiting for me in those shadows. I was right.

Out into the next street - I had lost my bearings but it didn't matter for now as long as I kept him in sight - and to my left, his silhouette moving in and out of the street lamp spotlights as he ran down the sidewalk. I paced my stride now, and kept my breathing even. I knew I could run all night if I had to.

I didn't. He slowed to a fast walk, made a sudden turn to his right and disappeared up a wide staircase and through double swinging doors. I reached the same point and took the steps three at a time. I noticed offhandedly that the writing on the swinging doors said *Opera House*.

Abbie and I had attended a show here back in early December. The Sweeney-Coombs Opera House was an impressive four-story structure that took up much of its block. It had a canopy above the second floor windows, and an ornate parapet at its top. Inside were offices, theatre-related businesses, several apartments, equipment storage rooms and, of course, the opera stage itself.

Which at this moment was filled with an entire overdressed cast performing before a breathlessly silent full house. A woman's voice was lilting up to the diamond-clad balcony patrons, and a man was responding in deep, low tones that seemed to shake the rafters. My notion is that they were singing in German, one of several languages I knew and cared nothing about.

I was stopped at the foyer doors to the theatre. A man in a tuxedo smiled at me and put his hand out for my ticket. I looked past him, in toward the stage.

"I'm a detective," I said quickly and quietly. "A man just ran through here. He is a wanted felon." It sounded very official.

The usher smiled. "Yes, sir, he did in fact just enter the building." He pointed off to his right down the lobby. "He headed that way. He was breathing very hard, you know. I assumed he was ill and directed him to the toilet. At the end of the hall."

I was already moving. I pushed open the door that said *Gentlemen* and stepped inside. I had my hand on my pistol but in that close range and a public place a gunshot seemed a bit much. Still.

He wasn't in there. It was empty. I stepped back out to the lobby, looked down at the usher who had watched my progress. I shrugged at him. He smiled.

A sudden rush of noise told me that the play had reached intermission. The applause lasted a full minute as I looked through the closets and hat check room at the far end of the lobby. Not there. The crowd began to pour out from the theatre and the foyer filled to overflowing. Damn. He could vanish in the crowd.

Before they reached me I opened one last door, the one that swung out to the far wall of the building. It led to a narrow aisle that seemed to head back behind the stage. It was dark except for a lone lamp that hung about halfway down the way, throwing more shadows than light. I felt along the walls as I made my way. Felt no other doors, no compartments, no other exits. Kept moving forward. Came to another door, likewise narrow. Pushed it open carefully. I was backstage.

I heard movement to my right, toward the main stage itself. Shoved through boxes and crates that littered the floor. Felt curtain and set ropes along the wall to my right, saw the stage lights ahead of me, maybe another twenty paces. A thick, black side curtain draped down to my left. Another movement just on the other side caused the curtain to billow just slightly. Reached with my left hand to the edge of the drape, pulled it suddenly toward me, swung my right arm around to grab the intruder.

A gasp in the darkness. A high-pitched one, at that. My hand gripped the arm of a beautiful woman, heavily made up, bright red lips, her hair cascading down in ringlets to her shoulder bared above a shimmering blue gown. Her eyes were wide open in fear. I relaxed my grip, mumbled an apology of sorts, and walked past her. She hurled "brute" at me as I moved on. Probably practicing her lines for Act Two.

The remainder of the opera cast had wandered off stage and stood about in various size groups. Some were talking, others adjusting costumes, others lighting up cigarillos during the respite.

None paid any attention to me, thinking I was just a stage hand doing my business.

I walked out onto the main stage, the curtain down and to my right. At this range the already exaggerated set looked more so, glittered and gilded and much too large to be real. I stood in the center and moved my gaze from end to end slowly, cautiously, looking past who and what was there, looking for what wasn't supposed to be there.

I spotted him on the second sweep. To my right, over on the other side of the stage, behind a black drape. I could see the heels of his shoes in the inch that separated drape from stage floor. It could have been another actor, but there was something peculiar about the shoes: they weren't peculiar. Not high heeled, nor oversized, nor glittered. Regular shoes.

I stepped quietly along until I was right behind him, separated by the backdrop. I drew my pistol, guessed the approximate height of my adversary from the spotty moments I had seen him during the chase, and brought the butt of the revolver down hard against a fold in the curtain. I could feel the crunching sound shiver through my arm and into my shoulder. Then the slump of clothes and body as he crumpled in a heap to the floor.

I walked around the drop and knelt beside him. He lay moaning quietly, his arms and legs spread out in odd directions. His hat lay two feet away. I saw no red hair, just dirty black. I holstered my gun, heaved him over onto his back. His arms and legs came along and more or less straightened themselves out. He was still moaning, not unconscious but the pain throbbing at the back of his head awful enough to wish he was.

I slapped him across the face. Hard. He shook his head. Opened his eyes. Wide. I grabbed a fistful of collar and throat and dragged him six feet over and against the stage wall. I sat him up roughly, my hand still on his larynx, pushing enough to gag him and get his attention. I waited for his eyes to focus. It took a few moments. I leaned into his face until our noses nearly touched.

"You were following me," I said plainly. "Why?"

"You got the wrong fella, mister," he gargled. I pinched my fingers into his throat. He made a strange sound.

"I don't think so. I think it's the other way around. You picked the wrong fella to follow."

"He paid me to keep an eye on you, that's all, mister," he managed.

"Who? I need a name."

"Don't know his name, I swear." I squeezed again. He gagged. "I swear, mister," he repeated. Damn, I believed him.

"How does he contact you? How do you report in?"

"He just shows up, I never know when or how he finds me. He's just there at my place, or a café. You know."

"How often do you report in?"

"I don't know, every day, I guess." He was gasping for each breath.

"Can you get a message to him?"

"I don't know. I guess." I squeezed. "Yeah, sure, okay. Please, that hurts."

"You tell him I'm waiting for him. No more goons. No more shadows." I squeezed for good measure. He tried to swallow. It seemed to hurt. "He knows how to find me. You tell him to find me. Do you understand?"

"Sure, mister. You gonna let me go?" No, you dumb ass, I'm going to kill you and then have you give him the message. I sighed.

Stood up, lifting him by the throat to his feet. He gurgled something, probably that he didn't like that. We were leaning against the curtain ropes on the other side of the stage from where we had entered. I looked at the long line of ropes and pulleys in front of me. Chose one, hefty-looking, pulled down on it for some give. It was heavy and hard to pull. I jerked on it again, and noticed off to my right that the main stage curtain jumped when I did that. Hmm. I jumped a few inches off the floor and grabbed at the rope as I high as I could reach, pulled down hard, his throat still in my left grip. The rope gave enough that time and some slack appeared briefly. I wrapped the rope around his throat, dropping my grip at the same time.

The rope tightened again, and his eyes bulged like they would pop right out onto the floor. His tiptoes barely touched the stage.

"Enjoy the show," I said, patting him on the chest. I left. When intermission ended, I figured his screams would interrupt the show for a moment while they untangled him. Good theatre, that.

I returned to the Rice Hotel to find Abigail closely guarded by a police detective situated outside the door. I dismissed him until dawn and spent the night recounting very little of what had happened. At dawn I had her packed and gone with the officer who showed up for duty, off to a secret hideaway where she would be safe. I promised her I would be all right. She seemed doubtful.

I went back to Beaumont that morning, Friday, January 10. I got to Big Hill about 10:30.

I was two hundred yards from the derrick when I felt the earth rumble beneath my feet as I walked the rutted road from town. I'd never felt anything quite like it before. I stopped and stared forward.

A roaring sound was accompanied by a blast of mud and rocks up through the derrick platform floor. I watched as the four men standing on or around the rig flew through the air, one of them dumped into the sludge pit and disappearing for an instant below the muck.

The last drilling pipe, still above the surface and attached to the pump with chains and pulleys, shot up into the morning sky, through the crown and off at an angle, ripping itself from the rig attachments and tearing at the tower itself as it did. Then came the next twenty-foot pipe, out of the ground and into the air. And the next. And another. One after another they came, like giant arrows shot from Hell. They careened in all directions as they crested above the rig, landing with a thump and imbedded into the ground.

In between came more mud and huge rocks that must've ripped the hole wide open. The rocks flew farther than the pipe. The four men at the base of this eruption could only lay flat on the ground and cover their heads, hoping they would not be driven into Big Hill by one of the projectiles. One shower of stones came within twenty paces of where I stood frozen in place.

For twenty, thirty seconds the blast roared on, the hill shook, the mud and whatever else it carried spraying the sky and the soil beneath it.

And then it quit. Just as instantly as it had begun. A final gob of muck trembled to earth with a splat.

The shock wore off and in that same instant I was on a dead run for the rig. Al and Curt Hamill and their brother Jim were slowly coming to their feet, testing bones and limbs for damage, rubbing mud off clothes and foreheads. My friend Peck Byrd sloshed his way out of the sludge and was a helluva sight. In the few seconds it took for me to cover the distance, I arrived as all four of the crew stood in unison, hands on their hips, staring up at the broken crown of the derrick tower. I did the same.

Al reached for a shovel laying at his feet and took one scoop at a pile of rocks in front of him. Peck said to no one in particular, "Now what the hell are we gonna do?"

In the next frozen second of time, I gazed over Big Hill. The world seemed to slow down. Three boys on horseback sat uneasily about four hundred yards down the hill, while another lone rider sat astride his mount across the way. The sky was cold and blue, not even a wisp of a cloud anywhere, the temperature hovering just above freezing, the last vestige of a hoary ground frost still in the shade. Not a hint of wind. Like the world around Big Hill was holding its breath.

And then I guess the whole world changed.

Without any forewarning this time, no rumbling earthquake, a sound like a twenty-pounder cannon went off, split the air, rocked and echoed for miles. All five of us at the rig shut our eyes against the sudden blast like that would fend it off. An instant later we opened our eyes. And our mouths probably fell open.

A geyser of dark green oil rose from deep in the bowels of the earth, shot straight up and through the broken crown of the tower, and rose another hundred feet into the Texas sky. There it sprayed out like an umbrella tearing apart in a terrible windstorm. And headed back to earth. And those of us standing beneath it.

We never even tried to move out from under it. Couldn't have, anyhow. It poured down on us, first like a bizarre sprinkle, then more of a shower, then almost like someone was pouring a bucketful right on our heads. We couldn't help ourselves, looked right up into it, winced and hollered as the thick stuff pelted our faces and got into our mouths and eyes. Blinded for a moment, I reached for a kerchief in my pocket and rubbed the stuff away as best I could.

Backstepping and stumbling, the crew and I made our way from the platform, ten paces, then fifty yards and ran fifty more until we reached the edge of the green-black shower.

Now I could feel the tremor from below, like the earth was pumping, throbbing.

I remembered a soldier on Kettle Hill who had been shot in the thigh as we ran together to the crest of our objective that July day. He had somersaulted forward and come to a halt sitting up, his rifle thrown to one side. I stopped long enough to bend down beside him, check him for

whatever had knocked him down. The Spaniard's bullet had hit an artery
in his right leg. The wound was ragged. His pants torn as well as his skin.
And the blood spurted from that blown artery, six inches into the air,
spraying the rest of his leg, his boot, and the ground around where he sat.

I put my rifle down for a moment, clamped my right hand down,
hard, on his leg. I could feel the blood pumping, oozing, striking against
my palm as I tried to stop it. The soldier was screaming right in my ear,
something unintelligible and terrifying. I wrested the belt from his pants
and tied it off around his thigh, right on top of the blood flow. Pulled
it as tight as I could. He screamed louder. I slapped him across his jaw
and he stopped. I placed both of his hands on top of the belt and hollered
at him to push hard against it until a medic arrived. Stood up. Shouted
for a medic and pointed at the fallen soldier in case anyone was looking.
Grabbed my rifle and ran to catch up with Teddy and the others now
twenty-five paces farther up that godforsaken hill.

I looked around Big Hill. The geyser of oil had darkened the
day like a sudden eclipse. The boys on horseback were gone. The
other rider - a guy named Charley Ingalls who I had met a few
days earlier, odd fellow - was making a mad dash down the hill
toward town, hat in hand and waving it like a madman. Could
hardly blame him for that.

The Hamill brothers and Peck Byrd had run in different directions, and we all stood pretty much by ourselves in spots at
the edge of the oil spray, like sentries posted around a battlefield.

Peck was closest to me and I waved at him and shouted, "Ask your question again, pardner: what the hell *do* we do now?" He waved back and trotted over to my side. He shook my hand, I guess that made sense, and hollered above the increasing noise of the gushing oil.

"Ain't that the damnedest thing you ever seen?"

"Is this what happens when you guys strike oil?" I asked.

"Hell no!" he shouted, laughed. "Never seen anything like it!" I nodded. He leaned closer, still shouting. "Gonna go tell Captain Lucas!" I nodded again. "You wanna come?"

"No," I called back as he started away. "I'll stay here with the crew, see what we can do with this thing." He waved over his shoulder, and took off running down the road. I watched him for a few seconds, saw the Lucas house a thousand yards away in the distance, a tiny speck just off the road. I wondered if the captain had seen his handiwork yet.

I made my way to where Al Hamill stood. He still had that shovel in his hand, gripped tight, probably didn't realize it. He acknowledged my arrival with a half nod, kept staring at the pumping oil spray.

"What the hell do we do now?" I asked. Damn good question.

"I have absolutely no idea in hell," he finally said after several seconds passed. I knew nothing about this oil well business, except that if Hamill didn't know what to do we were probably in a certain amount of trouble. I guessed if we didn't put a cap on the thing all the oil we'd been looking for would spill out on Big Hill and be gone, and that would be that.

I've been wrong before and since. Never that wrong.

23

Friday evening, January 10, the Lucas well seven hours gushing. We all stood on the front porch of Captain and Mrs. Lucas' modest camp house. Dusk was settling in on Big Hill. Curt and Al Hamill were there with the Lucases, Peck Byrd and me. Jim Hamill was in town. Someone had gone looking for Pattillo Higgins but no word if he'd learned about the well yet. Along the road that connected Beaumont and the hill were hundreds of people, old and young, big and small, bundled up in coats and shawls, lined along the ruts and doing the same thing we were doing: staring at the geyser of oil that blew unabated into the sunset sky.

A couple of hours earlier a photographer had come riding up in his wagon at near breakneck speed, tumbled out onto Big Hill with a big box camera on a tripod. He spent thirty minutes finagling with his machine, taking pictures, then whisked away back for town. Those'll make some kind of money, I thought to myself.

Very little had been said by anyone in the hours since the explosion of oil. We made several vain attempts to shovel dirt and rocks up against the platform to stem the flow. But the force of the oil was too great, the sound too shattering, for any of us to stay near the wounded derrick more than a minute at a time. Rock and sand just spewed away or back into our faces when we tried to toss it at the gushing green stuff.

Captain Lucas had arrived within twenty minutes after getting the word from his wife. She'd called for him at the store in town and he had driven a hack pell-mell to join us at the site, catapulting himself to the ground as he arrived and rolling into a somersault at Peck's feet in his rush to be there. The Austrian engineer had said very little since.

I looked up into the sky as the shadows finished covering the ground, turned to Al and the captain who were off at the end of the porch.

"Gonna need some security at the derrick tonight?" I inquired and sort of volunteered at the same time. They both nodded at me. I tipped my hat in the direction of Caroline Lucas, partly in thanks for the meal she had mustered quickly an hour earlier to some very hungry, grimy men. Patted Peck on the shoulder as

I stepped past him. He grinned at me. I walked off the porch, went to work.

Saturday morning, January 11, twenty-five hours gushing.
Peck Byrd and I stood away from the platform, shoveling sand into wheelbarrows. We'd been moving a pile closer to the geyser, figuring that at some time we'd be able to cover it. Soaked to the bone in oil and mud, and damn cold, we just kept shoveling, wheeling the stuff a hundred yards, dumping, go again. We no longer paid attention to the noise, maybe we were deaf by now.

Then the funniest thing happened.

The gusher quit. Just like that. Petered out over about two minutes, down from the sky, the crown block, until it dribbled across the platform like the hot springs that bubbled up over in Mineral Wells. It got real quiet again. We looked at each other for a whole minute. Kinda held our breath.

"Well, honey," Peck Byrd said in the direction of the hole, "that was a real nice ride." He kind of bowed at the waist, then blew a kiss at where the oil had been rising from the earth. Grinned his big grin at me. I smiled back, shook my head. What a helluva experience that had been, I thought.

Never finished the thought. There was another tremor, another cannon shot, and the gusher started right up again. Right back through the busted crown, a hundred feet and more into the midday sky. Noise, green goo, that awful smell. Peck said later it had been a gas pocket or something that had caused it to stop. Damnedest thing.

It just kept on, all the rest of Saturday and Saturday night. I kept vigil until Byrd relieved me just after sunup Sunday. The crowds had gotten bigger every hour, then faded off during the night. It was freezing cold, and standing around staring at that thing made your feet and fingers go numb. Besides, you could hear it but not see it so well after dark, took some of the excitement out of it. Still, I guessed the crowd in the thousands by late Saturday afternoon, and knew there'd be twice that Sunday if the thing kept pumping.

The trains from Houston and New Orleans were making their routes and probably double time, and one of the Hamills told me that each train was arriving loaded to the gills with spectators, and I figured speculators, too. People coming in already from Arkansas. The telegraph offices in Beaumont were melting wire with the news. Captain Lucas had wired Galey up in Pittsburgh.

And I had wired Abbie. Well, I got word to her, anyhow, through the Houston police. They got the message to her at the safe house to come join me in Beaumont as soon as possible, and to have one of the detectives accompany her. I knew it was probably not a good idea, put her back in harm's way. But I needed her here with me, to be in on this phenomenon, to witness this strange new world that was being born on this hill. Mostly I just needed her. Selfish. Maybe stupid. Love had made me stupid.

She arrived on the Sunday Noon train with an armed escort whom I didn't know but thanked for his time. He offered to stay. I declined. He waved and stayed on the train. Abbie stepped down onto the platform and into my arms. I gave her my very best hug.

She balled up a fist and hit me as hard as she could - very hard - on the front of my left shoulder.

"Ow! Damn!" I managed as I rubbed the spot. She was frowning at me.

"I hope this is worth that trip," she began, her tone somewhat less than gentle. "I've been squeezed in that car for four hours. It smells in there. I had hands all over me, and elbows and knees and god knows what else shoving and poking me." She took a deep breath. Wasn't quite done with me. "I have no earthly idea where my bag is," she motioned back behind her to the train. Steam whistled from under its carriage. "I haven't eaten today, rushed to the station, thought you were dying or something. Everyone panicked."

"I wanted you to see -," I began. She cut me off with her eyes, also with steam coming out of them.

"See what? Whatever this is, it had better be worth this." She looked around her. The depot was flooded with people, milling, pushing, waving, hollering. The mass dropped down onto the dirt streets and fanned out into the town of Beaumont. Every sidewalk was jammed with bodies, hacks could barely get through the streets, the drivers cursing and pointing as they made their way through it all. Men in suits called after the drivers, wads of cash in their hands, to get a ride out to Big Hill. It was chaos.

I cupped my hands over her ears, held her head in my hands, looked right into those eyes from an inch away.

"I'll make it worth your while," I whispered. Kissed her on the forehead, the tip of her perfect nose, tasted her lips for the first time in days. At first she did not respond. I caught my breath, held on. Then she kissed me back, full and deep and long. The thousands of strangers jostling us all disappeared for a moment.

"Why can't I stay mad at you?" she whispered between kisses.

"It's my boyish charm," I answered.

"Take me there," she said. I thought about that for a second. Oh, the well.

Abbie admitted it was worth the journey.

Sunday, January 12, Noon on Big Hill, fifty hours gushing oil. The ground along the crest and down one side of Big Hill had turned muddied from the oil. The dirt was dark and reflected a kind of shimmery green tone to it. Tumbleweeds and prairie grass long since covered up and gone, either from the oil or the trampling of thousands of shoes and boots and even the bare feet of children who had ventured out into the cold to see the spectacle.

Abbie and I stood some two hundred yards from the well. Peck Byrd and Captain Lucas were with us, a small entourage in a sea of strangers who moved in waves back and forth against the edge of the spray's perimeter. A barbed wire fence off to one side had long since been destroyed by the pushing crowds. I had already spent time doing my own shoving, escorting - that was the nice term - the overly-eager back and away from the derrick. I kept a shotgun in my hand most of the time, not really to use it but to discourage the brave ones.

As we watched along with everyone else, two men stepped up to us from the long line of patrons winding down the road. Walter Sharp was in his finest suit and top hat, his bright watch fob dangling from its vest as always, a row of cheroots in a breast pocket and the eternal cigar stub chomped and bent in the corner of his mouth. I had only known him a short time but had never seen him actually light the thing up. Just chewed on it. All the time. Fingered the watch fob.

I didn't know the other man until Walter introduced him as his brother Jim. I shook his hand and liked him immediately. Good, strong grip. Wore a suit but it somehow didn't look as appropriate on him as it did on Walter. His cowboy hat was tousled and dirty and comfortably perched on a mass of brown hair. He wore a holster with two pearl-handled revolvers jammed in it, and swung a long leather duster back off his hips every so often, ready for action. I had the notion he saw a lot of action. Wouldn't mind having him beside me in a pinch, I mused.

He doffed his cap in Abbie's direction when Walter called her name.

"Ma'am," he said pleasantly in a strong, deep voice. She smiled at him. Probably stopped his heart a beat. She did that to men.

"Mr. Sharp," she replied.

"The captain thinks another hand might be needed with the crowds," he said to me. I didn't mind the help and said so. "I'll go with whatever plan you got."

"Not much of a plan," I said. "The crowds pretty much got the idea now, of where they're not supposed to be. But new folks showing up by the trainload."

"Yep," Jim Sharp said. "I've got a shotgun with me and a rifle I can bring up, if you think that'll help."

"Folks pretty clear on the subject when they see that," I agreed.

"Okay," he said. "I can be back here in a half-hour." He touched the brim of his hat and started away.

"Cale," Abbie nudged me with a hand and turned to look at the crowd off to our left. There was some discomfort in the way she said my name. I turned and followed her gaze. Less than two hundred feet from where we stood, where the oil had seeped into the ground at the edge of its own shallow lake, a man stood off and apart from the rest. He was staring right at us, no question.

He was taller than most, black suit, white shirt and stiff white collar, black tie, a gray holster at his waist, black boots. He had a gray Panama that sat down on his forehead in a kind of sarcastic manner. A thin cigarillo was pursed between his lips, his hands cupped around a match as he lit up. Even from that distance I could see the glint in his eye, the half-smile. The recognition of the moment.

The red-haired man.

I stared across the distance with all of the energy and force I could muster, if looks could kill, and instinctively put one arm around Abbie's waist, the other hand to the butt of my pistol.

And the red-haired man tossed the match. It hung suspended for a horrible instant in mid-air, then fell flickering into the black-green pool. There was a moment's pause as it came to rest on top of the oily surface of the hill, as if it might have thought better of it and gone out. Then a tiny blue flame appeared around the match stick, followed quickly by a larger, brighter flame that began to spread in all directions.

The man who had dropped the igniter stepped aside with a smooth, practiced stride. He moved quickly into a crowd of people nearby, never taking his eyes off of me. Then, with a smarmy grin I wanted to peel off of his face ever so slowly, he yelled, "Fire!" The people around him immediately began screaming, running, panicked by the word itself before even seeing the growing conflagration at their feet. Children were scooped up, men grabbed women's arms and hurried them off, a man on horseback nearly fell when his mount reared on its hind legs at the sudden noise and movement.

I took several steps in the direction of the red-haired man I now had nearly in my grasp, but in that same instant I lost him to the frightened mob. Abbie grabbed my elbow from behind me. I turned to see a look of desperation on her face. Maybe because of the fire. Maybe because she knew who we had just seen.

"Abbie, go with Captain Lucas," I spit the words out loud enough for him to hear them. "Go get help from town." Lucas nodded that he understood and took Abbie's hand. She tugged against him for a moment, her eyes on mine. "I'll be all right, darlin'," I lowered my voice and spoke only to her. "Go on." Tears had already sprung into her eyes as she finally turned away to the captain's urgent tugs.

I looked once more into the crowd where he had been only seconds earlier - nothing. I glanced back at the acres of oil in front of me. The fire had spread ten, twenty feet already, and grimy smoke began to circle up into the sky. The smell was palpable. Flames licked at the ground like a coyote lapping the last blood from a kill. The screams of women on the hill could be heard above the other shouts. Horses neighed their disapproval and yanked their riders away from the fire.

Jim Sharp and Peck Byrd were suddenly at my side, the three of us seemingly the only ones not running and shouting. Peck pointed across one angle of the flaming pond and I followed his line. Curt Hamill was a hundred yards away waving in our direction. I recognized him by the slicker coat he had, a twin to the one Peck was wearing. The morning had been cold enough to add any wrap available. Now the slickers might come in handy. Sure enough, Curt pulled the poncho off his shoulders and raced for the edge of the flames. Peck followed suit on this end of the pool, pounding the wide coat against the fire.

I hated to make the next decision. I wanted the red-haired man in a stranglehold or at the end of a gun barrel so badly I could taste it. If I fought my way into the crowd I might spot him. But the fire was hungrily devouring this slope of Big Hill and the ones who were staying to fight it were few. If it got to the platform the gusher was done for. If the wind shifted, Beaumont itself might be its next target.

"Jim," I hollered at the cowboy I had only just met, "let's take that side." I pointed off to the left. He shouted in agreement and we took off in a dead run, matching each other's long strides as we skirted the flames. Peck continued to beat the ground where we had been standing. We could no longer see Curt because of the rising smoke, but we knew he would never give up his end of the fight.

Down the hill from where the derrick stood spilling more oil onto the soaked and now deadly ground, a wooden barn, more of a shack, had been a storage bin for our tools during the drilling. It stood maybe eight feet high and fifteen feet squared. I had no blanket or coat to beat the flames, no shovel to suffocate the fire with dirt, but I did have an idea. I communicated to Jim Sharp with hand signals for him to keep his post by the fiery lake while I went for the shanty. I ran the forty yards to the barn and kicked open the makeshift door.

Inside were piles of chains and two broken pulleys, three bales of hay - those would surely be no help, and the handle of what had once been a shovel or an axe. I grabbed the handle, stepped back outside and began to smash it against the side of the small building. The shed put up very little resistance and as the nails popped out from my hammering, the two by fours began to creak and twist apart. I created a small stack of lumber in just a few moments, threw down the handle, and picked up an armload of the wooden planks. The roof sagged: it was my next target.

I dragged the pieces of wood up the hill - it had been a damn sight easier to come down to the shack - and tossed them one at a time onto the spreading flames. The first one sort of bounced and made no impression on the fire monster's hide. But the second one I threw down did, dousing a narrow trench of yellow tongues.

I looked up to see Jim Sharp angling down to the shed, having watched my little experiment. Soon he came lugging up the hill, bearing off at an angle to deliver the load to Peck Byrd, I supposed. I was too busy with my own corner of hell to pay much attention. In a few minutes here came Sharp again, tirelessly moving, loading up, making his way up the hill with more lumber. I didn't know how long the shed would last, but it was better than doing nothing. I discovered that most of the two by fours could be used over again, one side charred but not in the fire long enough to disintegrate. I knew Peck and probably Curt would be doing the same.

The heat was growing unbearable and the smoke suffocating. I tried to stay generally upwind while at the same time moving with the edge of the fire as it set the gusher for a target. I pulled off my jacket, beat the flaming ground a dozen times with it until it was only a tattered rag, and threw it behind me. Did the same with my shirt and then my undershirt. Sweat and grime poured off my face and neck and down my chest. I just kept at it. The heat seared the hair on my arms and stomach as I fought.

It had seemed like hours but had probably been ten minutes before I stopped long enough to survey the larger scene. The smoke billowed high into the air now, and the fire had lapped up nearly an acre of land with plenty still to go. I could make out the ghostly silhouettes of more men who had come to help, saw Peck Byrd up the hill and Curt Hamill now at his side, both bare-chested, slamming blankets and boards to the ground. Someone had started a water brigade across the way and it seemed to be having an impact on the firestorm.

And then, peeking through a sudden opening in the sooty cloud bank, I saw two things that made my stomach turn and my heart come to a stop. One was the red-haired man standing directly across the lake of fire from me. The other was a large man who appeared to be his companion, standing at his side with Abbie firmly in his grasp. She was struggling to free herself from his arm around her waist but she was no match for his strength. She kicked and flailed and her fingers almost reached his face but fell just short. He stood there as if he were holding a rag doll.

I didn't think any of them had seen me. I dropped the length of lumber that I held and broke into a run at an angle that would take me around the fire and put them in range of my pistol. I lost them in the smoke after a few paces and hated the fact that I could not see them. Would they even be in that spot when I got there, I wondered to myself as I ran. I had no choice except to make that spot and work from there.

My gait was steady and strong, even strides as I passed up several firefighters including Curt and Peck, both of whom barely glanced up as I ran by. I could tell with sideways looks that the teams were making some headway against the ground fire, taking control of three sides while the fourth - the most dangerous - crept closer to the Lucas well. The spray that still blackened the sky after more than two days could become a two hundred foot flame with just the slightest encouragement from the wind that still blew favorably. But the fire was creating its own windstorm and it would eventually find its target. I knew the others would be working to stop it. I had another visitor from hell to contend with first.

I came to a point around the corner I had aimed for, and slowed to a walk. Ten paces. Stopped. Smoke and smell and noise and heat was the whole world where I stood. Pulled my pistol from my hip. Cocked, held at my side. Peered through the haze. Saw ghostly figures some forty feet in front of me, one, then two more. Was it him? I couldn't tell. Was Abbie there?

A sudden wind shift, as the fire sucked in its breath. The smoke vanished in an instant. The four of us stood in a pocket of clear air, inside a smoky bubble while the inferno raged around us.

And inside of me.

The trio stood in the same configuration as when I had first spotted them. Waiting for me. All right, I'm here now.

The red-haired man spotted me first. His compadre followed the gaze in my direction. Abbie continued to struggle, her head turned away from me. The broad-shouldered thug smiled a toothy grin while his employer managed only a turn in one corner of his mouth. Abbie sensed something had happened, stopped her writhing, tilted her head around until she saw me. Froze.

"Let her go," I called across the space that separated us, loud enough to be heard over the fire that consumed the prairie just a few feet to my left. Kept my arm down at my side.

"Can't do that, Lincoln," the mysterious stranger called back.

"What do you want?" I asked.

"I want you," he shouted.

"You have me," I noted, spreading my left arm out from my side, palm open.

"I have both of you," he almost smiled. Good point.

"Me for the girl," I said, knowing how well that would go over in this negotiation.

"Not good enough," he shook his head slightly.

"You don't need her. She doesn't know anything." We all knew better, except maybe for the pugface who held her.

"Sure she does," the stranger replied. "You're the last connection. We can finish it here." I knew we would, one way or the other.

The fire exhaled.

Smoke began to gather between us. The colors gave way to gray, the identities to phantasms. The temperature rose quickly. So did the edge to the moment.

The red-haired man raised his hand from his side. I could see the gun as he turned it toward Abbie's head. She couldn't help but stare right into its murderous barrel. The thug held her still.

Two things happened in the next second.

Abbie slumped in her captor's grasp, her deadweight dropping her toward the ground.

And a spray of red appeared on the sidekick's face and throat. His eyes widened in surprise, his fingers let go of their prey, and his shoulders stiffened. In the next instant I heard the sound of the gunshot, off to my right and behind me. I looked quickly over my shoulder and through the thickening smog.

Jim Sharp was lowering his shotgun from his shoulder, his eyes still fixed on his quarry. A second shot would be instantaneous if necessary.

I looked back toward the trio. Abbie lay on the ground, her eyes concentrating hard on me. The thug was falling backward in slow motion, blood covering his head and neck already.

And the red-haired man was gone.

I took two steps forward as I raised my pistol in the same motion. The infernal smoke hampered my vision, but he couldn't have gone far, dammit. A rush of noise as the fire beside me took another awful bite from the prairie grass. A wall of heat slapped the side of my face and my bare arm.

Then I saw him.

He had stepped to his right as the shot had sounded, and was inching backward now, his pistol raised in my direction. His expression never changed.

This was the moment both of us had expected to come. One of us was about to die. I didn't expect it to be me.

A hush descended as the rest of the world came to a sudden halt around us.

We fired at the same instant, each getting off two quick shots. His first bullet whipped across my right cheek and left a bleeding line like a razor had cut me. The second bullet, not a half breath behind, caught me in the upper right shoulder and spun me around. I managed to toss my revolver into my good left hand before it fell to the ground. I let the momentum spin me all the way around until I faced him again, dropping to a crouch in the same motion and raising the gun in his direction.

Both of my bullets had found their target, the first smashing into the collarbone on the left side of his neck, missing his throat by two inches. The second bullet drove high into his chest, piercing vest and shirt and skin and bone on its path.

In that frozen instant of time I expected to see him topple backwards from the two fisted strike. Instead, he slid his right foot back to regain his balance, and stood straight as a fence post, dark crimson fluid already staining his chest.

I raised my pistol in my left hand, the pain from being shot only a moment away. We would finish it here, now.

Then the red-haired man lowered his pistol, his eyes wide and round and angry, looking right at me and through me. He glanced to his right without moving his head. And stepped into the wall of fire.

I was too stunned to pull the trigger. He simply vanished. No shout, no hesitation.

"God damn you," I whispered as the smoke enveloped the moment.

24

February 2, 1901

We walked from Jim Baker's law office down to the
bayou bridge and found a stone bench to sit on. It was
shivering cold even though the sun shone. A breeze from the
north reminded us that the Texas winter was not done with us
quite yet. Abbie had a green shawl wrapped tightly about her
shoulders.

An alligator maybe thirty inches long was sunning itself on
the banks of the murky brown water about ten yards from where
we sat. Nearby a bullfrog sat on its haunches, its eyes glued on
the gator. Neither moved a muscle. We watched without comment for two, three minutes. I held Abbie's hand tightly in mine.
She stroked the top of my wrist.

"Captain Baker is encouraged that the trial will go well," she said absently.

"Mm hm," I agreed.

"The evidence is strong for a murder conviction."

"Charlie's confession broke it open," I said.

"You were responsible for that."

"I suppose."

"You are thinking of something else," she noted correctly.

"I never even knew his name," I said.

"It doesn't matter now."

"It does to me," I said gently.

"He was burned up in the fire."

"Fires of hell," I mused.

"It's over," she offered another tack.

"When the trial is done," I said.

"Yes, when the trial is done." A minute passed. The gator rolled its eyes from the back of its head. "Will you return to New York City to testify?"

"To testify, uh huh," I replied.

"Will you take me with you?" she asked, her voice softer.

I turned to her eyes. "I will never let you out of my sight again."

"You are sweet and romantic," she said.

"And gallant," I said, emphasizing the second syllable.

"And I love you."

"That would be my hope," I answered. "Always," I added.

The gator moved its right front leg forward a half-inch. The bullfrog thought better of the staring contest, slipped effortlessly into the bayou and beneath the surface. Several seconds went by. The gator didn't move. Ten feet out into the syrupy slow current, two bulging eyes popped from the mire. Then disappeared again.

Epilogue

The final toll from the Galveston storm was set at six thousand. Most of the bodies were never identified, never claimed, or simply never found. Hundreds were taken by barge out into the Gulf and dumped; days later most of them floated on to the beaches. Great funeral pyres lit the island skies for weeks thereafter.

The Lucas well at Spindletop was capped on the ninth day after it had erupted. It was estimated that 700,000 barrels of Texas crude oil had spilled to the ground before the Hamills got control of it. The population of Beaumont doubled in days, and doubled again and again in the months that followed. The boom continued in southeast Texas for the next three years. The petroleum industry was never the same.

Albert T. Patrick and Charles Jones were found guilty of murdering William Marsh Rice and both served time in the state penitentiary. Patrick, the chief conspirator and brains behind the diabolical plan, was eventually released for good behavior and, in 1912, granted a full pardon by the governor of New York.

On September 23, 1912, The Rice Institute opened its academic doors in Houston, Texas.

Made in the USA
Columbia, SC
20 November 2023

26498026R00183